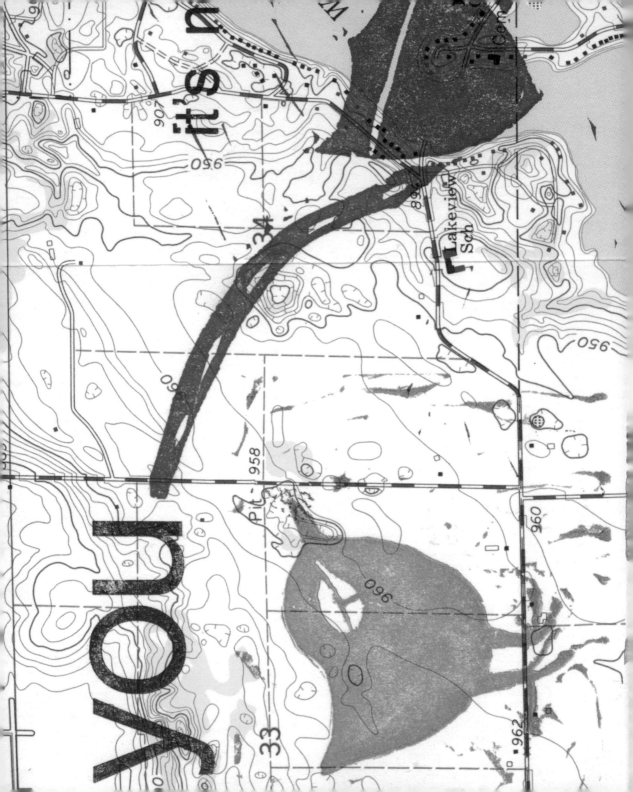

VIA AIR MAIL
LOS ANGELES, CALIF.
Miss E. Elizabeth Heydt.
Slatington Pa.
PALM
FEB 6 7AM 1912 PA
MARINE CORPS SCHOOLS, VA
JUN 14 AM 1967
50TH ANNIV
MARINE CORPS
29 AUG. 1916
RETURN TO
TO THE GIRL OF MY DREAMS

OTHER
PEOPLE'S
LOVE
LETTERS

150 Letters you were

150 Letters

NEVER MEANT to SEE

edited by
BILL SHAPIRO

CLARKSON POTTER/PUBLISHERS
NEW YORK

Copyright © 2007 by Bill Shapiro

All rights reserved.
Published in the United States by
Clarkson Potter/Publishers, an
imprint of the Crown Publishing
Group, a division of Random House,
Inc., New York.
www.crownpublishing.com
www.clarksonpotter.com

Clarkson N. Potter is a trademark
and Potter and colophon are
registered trademarks of Random
House, Inc.

Library of Congress Cataloging-
in-Publication Data
Shapiro, Bill.
  Other people's love letters /
Bill Shapiro. — 1st ed
    p.   cm.
1. Love-letters—United States.
I. Title.
HQ801.3.S53 2007
392.6—dc22   2007006764

ISBN 978-0-307-38264-1

Printed in China

Design by Laura Palese

10 9 8 7 6

First Edition

To Sasha and Soren:

This is my love letter to you

INTRODUCTION

The first time I read a love letter that wasn't addressed to me, my heart danced a guilty little dance.

A confession: Not only wasn't the letter mine, but it was written to a woman I was dating. She was in her bedroom, deciding on shoes; I was killing time in her kitchen, nibbling almonds. On her counter, the usual mess: a few photos, an address book, small piles of bills. Perhaps I looked a little more closely than I should have, but atop one pile, seated like a king, was a love letter.

I picked it up, I did, and I can't say I'm proud of that. But once I did . . . well, there was no turning away. That love note, rough-edged and wrinkled, had a curious effect on me. Confusion, yes, and a hint of vulnerability, but something else too. What her other man had written—a year ago? ten years ago? I had no idea—felt strikingly similar to a note I'd scratched out to her only a few weeks before. Not the words, exactly, but that flood of emotion, the playfulness, the optimism. It all seemed so familiar. A question twittered in my mind: Was our relationship as special as I had thought? At the same time, his note was clearly his own, with its inside jokes and (vividly) spelled-out desires. In fact, I could hardly believe it was written to the woman I thought I knew. I read it twice.

Three times, actually.

I WONDERED WHY SHE HAD LEFT IT THERE. IT WAS PROBABLY BY ACCI-
DENT. But it also could have been by accident-on-purpose, in which case what was she
telling me? Had he touched something in her that I hadn't? Did he mean something to her
that I didn't? And then the bigger questions swooped in: What role did this letter play in
her life? Was it something she had unearthed to remind herself of how good love can get . . .
or how fleeting it can be?

Why, in short, had she saved this nine-line scrawl? And was she so different from everyone
else? I began to consider what these much-folded pieces of paper might symbolize for us,
emotionally; why some we toss within moments, why we hang on to others for decades. Is it
because each letter from an ex represents a road not taken? And each letter from the person we're still with reminds us of what brought us together? Or could it be because a love
letter recalls that moment in our life when someone saw our best self?

SO I STARTED COLLECTING OTHER PEOPLE'S LOVE LETTERS. I contacted everyone I
knew, and asked if they would send me any they'd been keeping. Eventually, I even assembled
a team of researchers to do more legwork (these brave souls went so far as to call their
exes . . . who called *their* exes) until the web expanded far beyond our own circles.

I wasn't interested in the kind of correspondence typically found in love letter collec-
tions. Not the quill-tip pen variety that Ben Franklin sent to Mrs. F during their
courtship. I sought love letters, e-mails, text messages, and postcards written by regular
people in relationships probably much like yours. And who wants to look only at letters
that present bouquet after bouquet of love's red roses. Modern love is complicated. It bobs

and weaves, takes two steps forward, one step back. I wanted letters that not only captured the whispered promises of endless love, but also candid moments of uncertainty, bitterness, and regret. The thorns.

Envelopes began to arrive, each holding what, until the moment I opened them, had been a very private message. Inside the first, a tender apology. The second brought two single-spaced pages of triple-X lust. After that: "I'm not feeling what you're feeling." In the end, I had hundreds and hundreds stacked in my living room.

HERE'S SOMETHING I LEARNED ABOUT LOVE LETTERS: MOST DIE AN IGNOMINIOUS DEATH. They're torn up, tossed out, and fed to the dog. Burned, buried, and flushed. The letters on the pages that follow are the survivors. They were saved and savored. And, now, they're shared: Every letter here is printed with permission from its writer. ∎

Who wrote these letters? You name it: helicopter pilots, musicians, sociologists, sales reps, students, retirees, housewives, computer programmers, consultants, construction workers, architects, teachers, kids, lawyers, store clerks, filmmakers. The faithful and the adulterous. Maybe someone you know. Maybe your lover.

Gathering these letters provided me with a rare opportunity: the chance to freely poke through other people's intimate correspondence and not feel the least bit ashamed about it, as you might one day should you let your eyes wander for too long on someone's kitchen counter. After all, while almost everyone will get a love letter at some point in his or her life, it's unlikely to be passed around the dinner table. More often it will be squirreled away in the back of the file cabinet in a folder falsely labeled "auto insurance." (Note: If this is where you've been hiding yours, now might be a good time to rethink that.)

Like those still-hidden letters, the notes collected here were written only for a lover's eyes; they are unflinchingly honest. Reading them is like picking the lock on a stranger's heart and peering inside during the most intense moments of his or her life. But the fascination here is more complex than a simple case of voyeurism. Because, on a deeper level, the heart you're looking into is your own.

In a handful of cases, the letters are printed with the permission of the writer's closest living relative. Also, some letters have been slightly altered to protect the writer's identity or that of the recipient. One more thing: Not all letters are printed in their entirety.

I love that you
sent me an actual
letter.

I can feel your
hand on the pen,
pressing firmly
on the paper.

Did you moisten the
envelope with your
lips?

dan: I wanted to tell you
that I know you are
sorry - and that's all I
can ask from you. we've
all done things we are
sorry for - nor do I fully
blame you anyway.
we need time, but I
want nothing more than
to be your friend again -
when it feels right.
    love kerry.

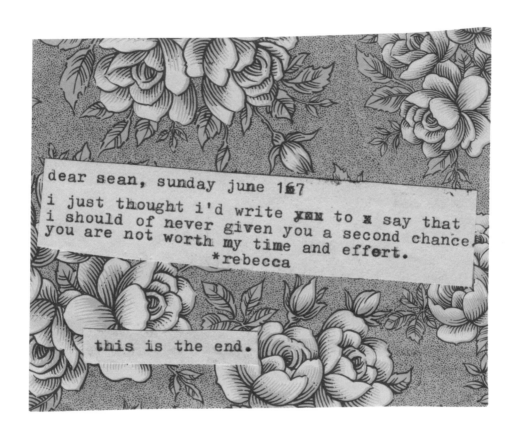

dear sean, sunday june 1~7
i just thought i'd write ~you~ to ~x~ say that
i should of never given you a second chance,
you are not worth my time and effort.
              *rebecca

this is the end.

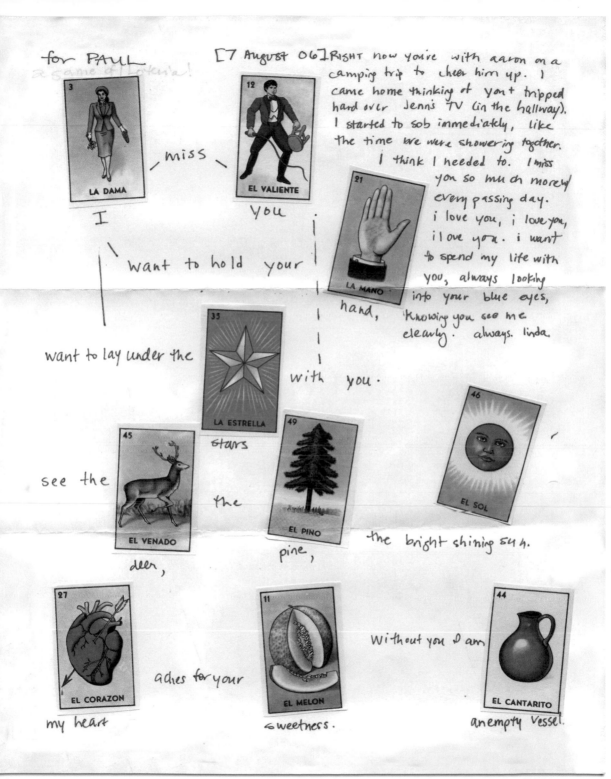

for PAUL
a game of Loteria!

[7 August 06] RIGHT now you're with aaron on a camping trip to cheer him up. I came home thinking of you + tripped hard over Jenni's TV (in the hallway). I started to sob immediately, like the time we were showering together. I think I needed to. I miss you so much more w/ every passing day. i love you, i love you, i love you. i want to spend my life with you, always looking into your blue eyes, knowing you see me clearly. always. linda.

3 LA DAMA

I

- miss -

12 EL VALIENTE

you

want to hold your

21 LA MANO

hand,

want to lay under the

35 LA ESTRELLA

stars

with you.

see the

45 EL VENADO

deer,

the

49 EL PINO

pine,

46 EL SOL

the bright shining sun.

27 EL CORAZON

my heart

aches for your

11 EL MELON

sweetness.

Without you I am

44 EL CANTARITO

an empty vessel.

I think UR great.
Wanna have wine & tequila again sometime?
HELL yes.
WHAT?
no.
UR THINK I'M CRAZY? yes! over

p.s. I look forward to your

Also, where do

letters too much to call.

you stand on chains?

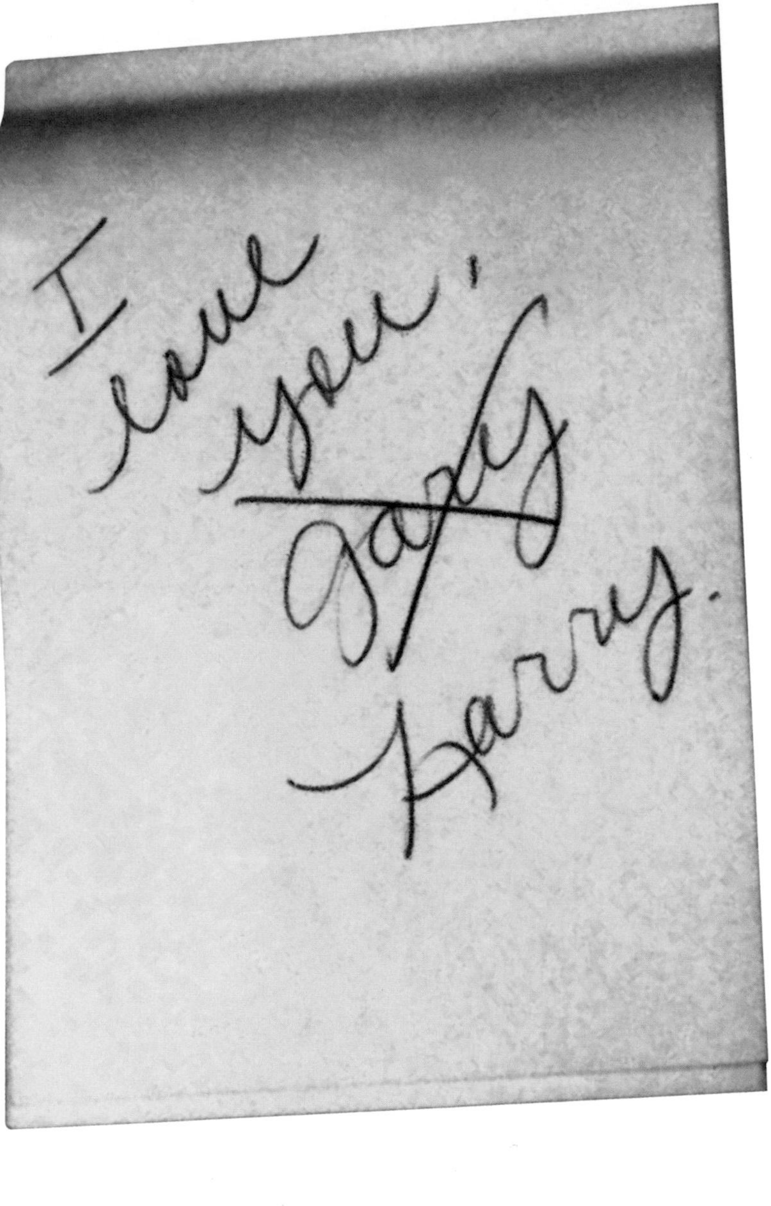
I love you,
~~Gary~~
Harry.

Thank you, I hate you, I'm sorry

Thank you
because without your support, I wouldn't be here
I wouldn't have stayed when things got hard
I wouldn't have believed that I could find a life.
Thank you for the way you know me,
for being my best friend for what feels like forever,
and for raising the bar so high that I don't know where to begin.
Thank you for knowing to let go before things got ugly.
On some level, you must've known that forcing me to fly
would force you to fly too, to do the things you know you need.
And maybe you even share the belief that our paths
will join us together again, and for always.

I hate you
for not wanting it badly enough,
for not believing we could do this together,
for not following through.
I hate that you didn't have the balls to take a chance,
to explore this place that's filled with your dreams.
I hate that you don't even seem to be doing
the things that made you stay.
I hate that the way you tell me how you feel almost always hurts,
and that most of the time you just don't tell me at all.
I hate that you are the only guy I can imagine loving,
and you make letting go seem so easy,
like it doesn't hurt at all,
like you don't ever cry.

I'm sorry
I left the way I did,
because of what it said to you:
that I would always expect you to follow.
I'm sorry I didn't see it like that.
I thought paving the way would create
an adventure that would change our lives.
I'm sorry I didn't wait until you were ready,
that I didn't think I could, so the decision didn't feel like yours.
I'm sorry that it seemed like your opinion wasn't important,
when nothing could be further from the truth.
I'm sorry that I doubted our future, and made you doubt it too.
I didn't know well enough myself to tell you
all the things that needed to change, and why.
We both thought we'd have more time, and then I left.
I'll always be sorry for that.

♡ — Mildred —

6:35 AM — Gone for my
walk. I'll be back about
7:25.

Love Don

Walking

Sunday AM.
11/18/90
7:10

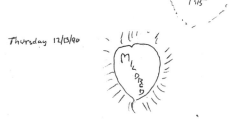

7:55 AM

6:35 AM Tuesday 10/30

Mildred +
a Waffel
7:15

Saturday
11/17/90
6:35 AM

MILDRED

HOME

7:10 AM

Thursday 12/13/90

MILDRED

7:05 AM

AM
7:40

9:20 AM Wednesday 12/5/90

MILDRED

7:35 AM

TUESDAY 3/12/91

MILDRED

6:50   7:25

Thursday 4/25/91

MILDRED

6:50   AM   7:25

Hi Lauren,

I was going to come and see you today but I decided it would be better to leave things with the sweet memories I have of last night. I had a wonderful evening - thankyou.

I read your letter and it was the most beautiful thing anybody has ever written to me - I shall really miss you.

Anyway I'll write soon, but until then I'll see you in my dreams

Lots of love

DAN

And I shall love you until I draw my last breath, and beyond.

You asked me to "give you a little something?" Well here it is: I'm giving you half my heart. I wanted to give it to you today—even though I'm spacy, a little bit sore in all the good places and still have absolutely no saliva—because it's what I feel and I know it's "real." I also know that tonight will be hard for you, and that there will be harder times to come for both of us. But right now, I just want you to know that last night was totally off-the-charts incredible for me in the most surprising and profound ways. Even as I write this, I can feel my heart (the other half) twinge and my skin tingle (those frissons again) when I think about how strangely, wonderfully comfortable I felt with you...so close, so calm, just lying there in the pre-dawn delirium, softly touching, bodies entangled. I want to use the word intimacy even though I know the professionals will say it can't be so because it's not a "real" relationship. All I know is that being with you was amazing. You're amazing. Really.

Oh, and as for the other half of my heart, I'm going to hang on to it and try to keep it in a safe place for a while. Maybe you'll let me know, someday, if you want it. And maybe, someday, I'll give it to you.

What I really feel...

If you were here now,
I would kiss you.
I would hold your hand and
look at you with wonder,
And then,
if you would let me,
I would kiss you again,
And again.
And again.

If you were here now
we'd get in trouble.
The stewardesses would have to
pull us apart, then send one
to sit up front and the other
in back.

We'd get a scolding at the
airport, an asterisk by our
names for future flights,
then released, promising to never
ever again, salsa dance with
~~the fasten seatbelt sign~~
the seatbelt sign on.

The filing time shown in the date line on telegrams and day letters is STANDARD

L68CC JG INTL

RP OSAKA VIA MACKAYRDO

EFM MISS TRINA LEVY

5225 14 AVE BROOKLYNNY

LOVING WISHES FOR CHRISTMAS AND NEW

THOUGHTS AT THIS TIME. ALL MY LOVE.

SYMBOLS	
DL=Day Letter	
NL=Night Letter	
LC=Deferred Cable	
NLT=Cable Night Letter	
Ship Radiogram	

at point of origin.   Time of receipt is STANDARD TIME at point of destination

YEAR. YOU ARE MORE THAN EVER IN MY

TADDY

504A DEC

Fr:Jen

Can i just tell you
that my mouth is
missing something

and i wish you were in it!

I did not remember the flowers...it will be 468.19.

Yeah, the house is too much to deal with right now. Just not sure how it would fit into this life. How are the divorce papers coming? I have a few things to say to you that I thought might be better said in writing...

The decision you made to end the marriage was, as you know, a terribly difficult one for me. I didn't want it and never would have chosen it myself. I still believe that there's great value and honor in the commitment I made to go through together whatever comes, and I am changed by the fact that that was not a commitment we shared in the end. It changes my sense of safety and trust in the world-- though I don't think necessarily for the worse. I can accept my powerless over people, places and things better somehow now; I feel less expectation; but it's been hard to let go of the dream that we would be together, working out the problems as they came. There's been a great deal of sorrow and tumult in my life this year as a result of your decision,naturally, and only now am I coming back to my "true self" in a consistent way. By that I mean, only now do I wake up every day and feel like myself again.

I know you know that this was a painful event for me. I am sure it was painful for you. I still have times when I just don't get it, but I'm learning to accept that I don't GET to get it all the time when it comes to other people's choices. (You taught me that.) I will grieve for a long time that I won't get to hear you in the other room singing to the pets; that I will never return to "the space" and the love and safety I felt there (although the safety was, I think, something I made up out of a need for it from my own childhood); that I won't ever get to make rosemary shortbread for our Solstice or see our child in your arms. These and MANY other things I will regret for a long time.

You gave me so many things,   and I am so very grateful. You taught me to make the effort to be kind; you showed me that it was worth it for the sake of love. You taught me how to check my strong sense of justice (and judgment) against the effects it might have on others. You taught me love is more important than being "right". With you I learned how to fight cleaner, how to talk things out better, and how to make a strong loving family out of nothing. These are priceless gifts that I will carry with me the rest of my life.

One more thing you did for me: you left, and I had to get through it. I have learned this year that my ability to handle what happens to me greatly exceeds my expectations. I thought I would die if you left me; I had this idea that I would crumble, that I'd have to go live with my mom and curl up in bed for months. This is so untrue, and I have some amends to make to myself for thinking so little of my strength. I did cry a lot and have some wild times, but I used the loss of you to write the best play of my life so far; I learned about men and made deep lasting friendships; I found support and just got the fuck through it, through something I really thought would destroy me. It really was my greatest fear, that you would leave; that's why I didn't listen well when you kept saying you hated being married or that you wanted out. I couldn't hear it cause I was too scared of it. I'm sorry about that. But once your greatest fear happens, you never have to have it again. You gave me that, that freedom from the fear of being left, and the calm of knowing that other people cannot make the world a safe place for you; I never have to expect that from anyone again, and be hurt and terrified when it doesn't happen.

Don't get me wrong. I do not admire the part of you that cannot deal with the marriage, and that chose to leave me by phone, and that seems to be able to do this with so little affect, etc, etc. I'm not saying that in my book what you did is ok or whatever. I'm not sure at all that I forgive you. But it has given me strength and focus and a sense of myself that I have never had, and I am so grateful for that.

Now, the point of all this: I need you to get this divorce papers shit worked out. I want my name back. I want to be responsible for just my life again. I want ▩ to be able to be with an unmarried woman. I feel it's your responsibility to take care of this, since this was your choice; I do NOT feel comfortable taking care of divorce proceedings on my own, although I will if you won't get it done. ▩ and I are considering moving in together in the next few months and I want us to be able to do it with this behind me. I'm not sure what's in the way for you re: getting this done; maybe it's just a pain in the ass to do, maybe there's a part of you that doesn't want to deal with the emotions of fully breaking ties. But it's time to do it if we're going to move on.

I love you, ▩, and always will, in a way that's specific just to you. I'm sorry our relationship had to evolve in this way, but I also feel like it's right, for whatever reason. I will miss so much about our life together; I feel it was a good life, with so much fun and good conversation and coffee and friends and love. I don't think I'll ever fully understand why you had to go but I am accepting it and I am learning that my capacity to love others is deeper and stronger than I thought...it surprises me to find that it hasn't been damaged, I'm open and still want to give, even if it's not to you. Thank you for all the lovely days of talking and laughing and crying over "I Was Meant For the Stage" in the kitchen in each other's arms. Please take care of this stuff so I can go.

Love

Molly

ROZ— YOU SURE LOOKED
GOOD IN THOSE SWEATS
TODAY. IT LOOKED SO
I COULD NOT CONTROL
MYSELF.

11/19/02

Dear Beautiful

Can you believe its been 2 months since I first set eyes on you. From that day forward my life has not been the same.

Its amazing that every moment we're together surpasses the last. I cant wait to see what the future brings

Truly yours

Phil S.

717

Many e... es...loaded, key-...der factory war-ranty. $16,900 or best offer. Call 717-566-9033 or 566-6840 after 6

JEEP '91 Chero miles, goes w wheel drive, i Call 717-238-

JEEP '89 CHE 4X4, 4.0 liter, runs-drives gr Call 717-243-8

JEEP '84 CHE dition, new mo sion, current or best offer.

FORD '99 Expedition, Eddie Bauer, 4x4, white, tan interior, well main-tained, winterized, great in snow, many extras, have 22" wheels, must sell, $16,995, 821-2109.

FORD '99 Expedition
Eddie Bauer, CD changer, leather, heated seats, air level suspension, all wheel drive, mechanic owned, dealer serviced, never off road. $14,000/firm. Call New Cumberland 938-8768.

JEEP '79 Wagon Factory emerge great conditio $2500 or best c

KIA 2000 SPC 4x4, auto, air, door locks, 55,0 Call 717-418-04

LAND ROVER ERY: V8 auto, CD, tow package condition. $17,9

LANDROVER 20 blue, 77,000 mile leather interior. $18,500. 717-24

MITSUBISHI 2 Sport, all optic Asking $11,500 o Please call 7

FORD '98 EXPLORER
4wd, red, 53,000 miles, loaded, sun roof. Very clean. $12,000.
Call 790-2229

FORD '97 Expedition

Great condition. Good Mileage. fully loaded. $14,000 negotiable. 717-243-1297

Miscellaneous............668
Yard Sales East..........669
Yard Sales West.........670

604 Auctions

AUCTIONEER Equipment Liquidators Warehouse. Your complete com-mercial auctioneers & appraisers. #RY-000117-L 233-5773.

610 Pet/Supplies

AMERICAN BULL DOG/PIT BULL: mix pups, red and brindles, ready fo Christmas, 4 left at $200. 3 males 1 female. Call 717-571 3976.

AUSTRALIAN SHEPHERD : Registere Christmas puppies, tails docked first shots. Ready. Males $225, Fe males $250. Call 717-334-5770

BASSETT HOUND puppies, AKC. Tri colored. Shots and wormed. Adorable. $400.
Call 717-865-4727

BEAGLE PUPPIES
Tri-colored, parents on premises shots and wormed. $175 each. Call **717-932-8944.**

BEAGLE Pups, AKC. 1st shot and wormed. 13 inch tri-colored. $200 - males and females 717-862-1089

---

must submit the ...ter of interest, ...andard application, ...certification, Act ...earances, copy of ...ipts. Salary based and qualifications ...ription and submit James P. Dull, ...t 3940 Peters ...Halifax, PA 17032. ...line is Wednesday, ...4, 12:00 p.m. EOE

ATION:

entary and High Equal opportunity ...00 per day to at either the high entary school. ...s: teaching ...nd up to date ...end standard ...ation, copy of ...ate, and copies ...ces to: ...d C. Zema, ...uperintendent, ...e. School District, ...and Reynders ...Box 7645, 7113-7645.

ANALYST
non-profit seeks

From: Anna
Date: November 16, 2003 8:34:32 PM EST
To: [redacted]
Subject: Re: so

I had a lot of fun with you, [redacted]. You are charming, intense, challenging and you have an excellent cock, but I just don't have any enthusiasm for engaging with a man who is in a relationship with another woman. Not to mention, a man who is willing to cheat on his woman. It was super for one
night, but not for anything more than that. I am not playing hard to get. I am simply being real and truthful. That is why I resisted passing my phone number to you.

I am just starting match.com with the hopes of meeting a person who is 100% available and interested in a juicy long lasting kind of relationship. The kind that comes with hot sex, true friendship, deep trust, honest commitment and eventually a few kids. At 34, this is where I am in my life. I have a lot to give a man, and I am not about to waste my time on dead-end situations.

The evening ended abruptly. No time to talk. If there is anything you want to share, please do send me a note. I am open to listening to your thoughts.

Kindly,
anna

January 8, 1999

Doe,

Happy Hanukkah, Merry Christmas, Happy
New Year and Happy Birthday! How
compact. I can't believe how time forges
on. It's like a clock with an hour removed each
time the hands go around. But you're always
there, right on time. Thanks for another year
of advice, chat, adventure, high drama and even
the occasional hedonistic episode. Functional,
dysfunctional, maybe symbiotic? Who cares.
I relish our relationship for what it is.
Here's to a lifetime of it!

Love,
Andrew

Yes, I'm that girl. The one who waits for the Hallmark holiday to tell the guy she's crazy about the things she wants to tell him every day, but can't get him to stay awake long enough to tell him. Never in a million years would I have though that the painfully resonating "you" on the other end of the line would belong to the person who I now can't imagine being without. Without you, I'd have no one to beat in dominoes, no one to show me the true importance of following a recipe, no one to make me laugh, make me giddy and make me fat. No one to challenge what I say, question what I believe and encourage me to stand up for myself. You mean so much to me... I'm insanely crazy about you. Well except when you use that forbidden phrase - Then I'm only a little crazy about you. I got butterflies the first time you kissed me, and they haven't gone away. I hope they never do. Love Teresa

I'm having terribly naughty thoughts again today, and I was wondering if you might want to hear about them.

Am trying to focus on work, but you know how that goes—I keep having these delicious new ideas.

Oh well, have a pleasant afternoon.

LIAR

(WRITTEN 193 TIMES)

LIAR - LIAR - LIAR - LIAR - LIAR - LIAR

LIAR - LIAR - LIAR - LIAR - LIAR

liar - liar - liar - liar - liar

liar - liar - liar - liar - liar

liar - liar - liar - liar - liar

liar - liar - liar - liar - liar

liar - liar - liar - liar - liar

liar - liar - liar - liar - liar

liar - liar - liar - liar - liar

liar - liar - liar - liar - liar

liar - liar - liar - liar - liar - liar - liar - liar - liar - liar - liar - liar - liar - liar - liar

liar - liar - liar - liar - liar - liar - liar - liar - liar - liar - liar - liar - liar - liar - liar

liar - liar - liar - liar - liar - liar - liar - liar - liar - liar - liar - liar - liar - liar - liar

liar - liar - liar - liar - liar - liar - LIAR - liar - liar - liar - liar - liar - liar - liar - liar

liar - liar - liar - liar - liar - liar - LIAR - liar - liar - liar - liar - liar - liar - liar - liar

This is a love letter.

I wrote it in my head a couple of nights ago. I was kicking around downtown, not wanting (another) drink and yet not ready to hop the D train. I walked myself along the slick sidewalks of Elizabeth, Mott, and Mulberry for a while, thinking, thinking, thinking, looking in the windows, and thinking.

The last 18 months have been incredibly hard for me. And they've been incredibly important. I have unpeeled my past and examined my motivations and looked at myself in ways that I couldn't have imagined doing two years ago. I know this sounds like cornball woo-woo hoo-hah, but I really, really can feel the growth—it's like looking at those pencil marks Dad used to make on the back of the bathroom door.

As I continue to look at who I am and who I want to be, my sense of what kind of person I want to spend my life with becomes ever more clear.

This is the part of the letter where you come in.

I love our spark, I love our banter, I love "22" and "R." I love that cherries make you smile and that you knew (sort of) who Johnny Gharbini was. I love the way you look in your high-heel shoes. But that's the easy stuff. I also love whatever it is about you that let's me be me—or, more to the point, whatever it is about you that helps me be a better me. I love your sensitivity and insights, your challenge and your passion. I love that you criticize me and make me look hard at myself. I love your brain. I love that you've actually tried one of Beyonce's moves. I love that you accept so little at face value and always look for more. I love that you can say you're sorry and mean it. I love that you bought me my favorite tie. I love that you ask not only for what you need but also for what you want. I love the E on your sweater and the twinkle in your eye. I love that you can make me smile *and* make me cry. I love that you're thinking about the role of jealousy in our relationship. I love that unnamed thing in you that allows me to be vulnerable in front of you. I love knowing that, if I wanted to, I could continue this list for at least seven pages. I love the fact that I don't know whether or not you'll give me shit for being such a sap.

I want to end this note with something I didn't share with you. Something about last Friday. Allow me to set the scene. Remember that delicious afternoon nap? Remember how much we needed sleep, and how even though the curtains were drawn, the room was still pulling in all that grey light? Remember how I woke you up? If you could have seen me during the 15 minutes before your wake-up call, you would have seen a man watching a woman sleep. You would have seen tenderness in his eyes. You would have seen a smile on his lips. And if you had looked super-super hard, you just might have seen the love growing in his heart.

NEW YORK 🍎

new york loves you!
and misses you!
and wishes you were
here!
oh no wait, that's me!
here's the key.
love you

BROADWAY
N Y C

WISH YOU
WERE HERE

NYC
SUBWAY
MAP

Sent: Saturday, October 08, 2005 2:46 AM
Subject: Re: You

Hi

I hope my invitation to go on a date after all this time didn't
spook you. I liked you the first night we hung out together and
you pawed around for my potbelly. The more I've learned over the
past year, the more I like. Just incase my train careens off the
rails on my way to Philly tomorrow,
I would like to share a few turns of my heart that I was too shy
to offer in the car.

I love that you are loyal and devoted to your family, friends and
little bat-like dogs. Your sculpture is Dali meets Tiffany,
delicate and strangely beautiful. Your voice, the pace, resonates
with a deep quiet place inside me. I like
talking on the phone with you late at night, even if it is about
stain and grout.

You are super handsome and I remember liking kissing you.
You read books.
You are sensitive.
I suspect you are a great dad.
You are tender.
You build things.
You make me laugh a lot.
You have a big, bright generous heart and a trailer home!

It's okay if you are not interested or available. I wanted to
whisper my secrets to you anyway. Whatever happens, I hope we are
friends when I have a squeaky walker and you have bamboo cane
(that doubles as a magic wand).

Thank you for the proper ride home.

Sweet Dreams.

Pipe Smoke

Date: Tue, 11 Oct 2005 00:46:15 -0400
Subject: Re: reality

That was the most loving rejection ever, Randy, thank you for
being gentle. I am glad I asked and I am grateful for your
clarity. All the cobwebs of wishing and wondering were blown away
by this gust of reality. I do truly believe that I will be
recognized by the person I am intended for, and if you don't
recognize me, then it is certainly not meant to be. (I like to
think that I won't have to resort to any "arm twisting" on my
journey to find my true love.)

I hope that your friend in California works out for you, if that
is what you want. I value your friendship and would like to
continue. If my crush rears her head again, I hope you
understand that I may have to disappear, but for now I feel
comfortable and at ease with the idea of staying in touch.
I do still want to take you to dinner (raw, of course) to say
thank you for all of your help with my renovations, but maybe we
better wait until I am actually living in my apartment before we
start munching carrots sticks in celebration. In the meantime,
when "California" visits, assuming she is "raw", I suggest you
take her to Pure Food and Wine on Irving. I think you will enjoy
it.

Warmly,

Peace Pipe

will yoo be my
wife?

THERE'S A WARM, FUZZY FEELING YOU GET WHEN EVERYTHING GOES JUST THE WAY IT SHOULD.

And that's the way I feel every time I look into your eyes or hold you in my arms.

If you want to know more about

how I feel about you, picture this:

It's 3:53 a.m.

and we're awake, and

IT'LL TURN YOU ON, or maybe not.

And that's what I love about you, about us - I love how complete our relationship is + how complete you make me feel. Its unlike anything I've ever experienced....

to be continued....

. . . . because you'll

try anything once

mi flor,

together growing

growing together

heartsmiles spreading

truth neverending

love always beginning

in the joy of we

welcome the

discovery boundless

and wowful

sweetness and

powerful.

i love you.

To My Darling Husband—

Who would believe that almost four decades have passed and my love for you is still the focus of each and every day of our lives.

Many years ago you told me that you would always be my best friend. At the time I thought that statement was cute but somewhat meaningless — How wrong I was! Throughout all these years you have been not only to be my best friend, but my champion, my lover, my advisor, my buddy, my cheering squad and my support for all the myriad of incredible situations that constantly occur.

I cherish all the moments we share and hope that the next decade of years is kind to us so that we can celebrate our lives together and reap the goodness we constantly seek.

Know always that I love you and feel complete as your partner in life.

From: Maria
Date: Mon, 10 Oct 2005 14:44:38 -0400
To: David
Subject: Re: Commincia La Commedia

Hi, David:

I hate to do this, but I'm afraid I have to renege on Wednesday night. I searched my conscience and decided it might not be the best idea to meet up with you. I totally enjoyed your company the other night—you're smart, sweet, all those wonderful things--and I have no doubt that I would have lots of fun with you, but I don't think the chemistry thing is there for me. If only one could ordain these things.

I'm sorry (really), because I know I'm the one who will be missing out.

All best,
Maria

11 June 69

My E,

On the occasion of my being made aware of the birth of our first born, a son, the biggest feeling within me was one of elation. But even more than that is the feeling of thanking God for you. You who make up my whole life, love, and reason to be. Just think, Ellen, we have a son.

I love you so much. I'm so lucky to have you

for my wife! I love our baby so much. I hope your mother isn't too disappointed that it wasn't Sara Beth, maybe next time! You'll have to forgive me but I've been down the O-club for awhile and I'm a bit tipsy but I don't care because I'm filled with so much for you I could bust. I wish I was with you now. I'm so proud! I passed out cigars and got handshakes and congratulations. Ellen I love you. I'll write again as soon as I get back on the wagon. Oh how I love you My E. and my son Jock

My heart is wrinkled and brown. Inside it's not soft like dough. But it's given to you So there's nothing to But enjoy me, the best wife around. Love, M. 2·14·98

Tuning Fork

I'm yours. You're mine
Hear bells?
It's Valentine
tine
tine

♥

Dear Max,

I just heard from my lawyer that you and Phyllis are pressing ahead, suing me for support. I would like you to know why I think this action is unreasonable.

1.   I make $60,000 a year. I have been living in two very expensive cities since we separated—LA and Santa Barbara. While I have been able to support myself on my salary in these two locations, I do not have excess money to support you.

2.   We agreed many months ago that neither of us would seek support—of any type--from the other. I have emails that show it. I thought you would stick to this agreement.

3.   You are an able bodied, smart, talented person. You may not be able to get a management position in this economy, but you could certainly find some kind of work that would pay you as much per month as you are suing me for.

4.   To the extent that I do have any disposable income, whatsoever, I have other commitments that make considerably more sense than supporting an able-bodied adult like yourself. For example, I am taking Jesse on her east coast college trip in March. This will not be inexpensive, but because her mother has no money to spend on a trip like this, I have volunteered to pay this expense.

5.   I have already supported you in many ways over the past several years while you were unemployed. I paid many thousands of dollars in taxes. I put money into the house. I paid you $4000 in December. I paid for some medical bills. I enabled you to have health insurance, for free for six months after our separation.

6.   My credit rating, like yours, is shot. I have suffered from this house debacle like you have.

7.   I believe that you would not be in this dire financial shape if you had made an earlier decision around the house, if you had tried to get other work besides high-paying management positions long ago (as I encouraged you to do while we were still married, and to which you very emotionally responded, saying that I didn't believe in you if I encouraged you to do such a thing).

I do not understand what you are doing. I would like you to stop causing both of us more financial harm (lawyers' fees, etc). This is vindictive and ugly.

Still

Still

I'm surprised and
somehow know
I want when
I don't

Still

I really
missed you.

Still

Still

I [love] I

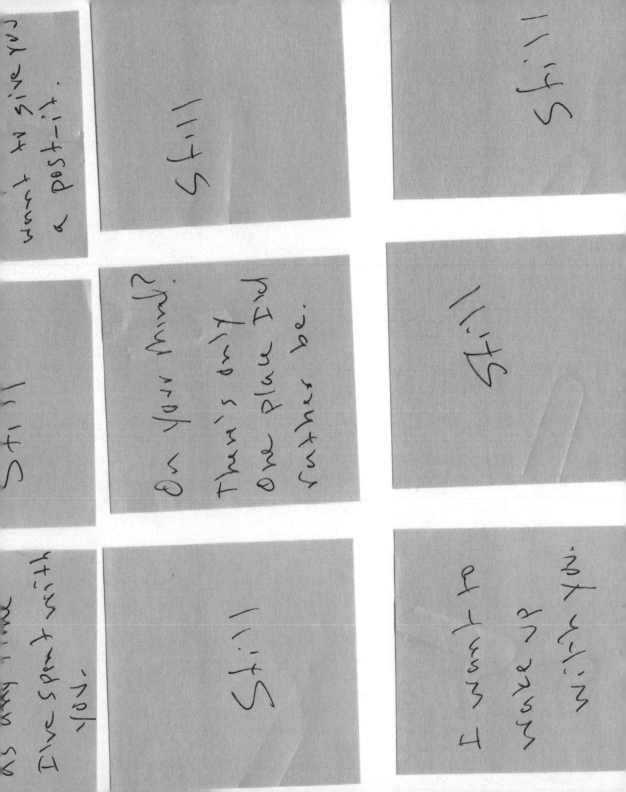

There once was this girl who was very, very good. She was blonde and pretty and got hit on relentlessly from the time she was 13 years old, but she, for various reasons, didn't lose her virginity until she was 24. She slept with only one more man after that, and then she moved to NYC, and met HER man. She stayed with him for 10 years, and thought they would always be together. She never cheated, strayed, looked elsewhere, even though the man, in the last few years of their relationship, gave her ample reason to do so because he really didn't seem interested in sex. She took it as a sign of being in such a long term relationship, and while it bothered her extremely, she wasn't going to give up a good, solid man and be cast out into the wilds of singledom in the city just for a little more sex.

But gradually, she began to lose sexual interest in her man as well, and soon she was 35 (a woman's sexual peak, remember) and looking at a long, dry, sexless road ahead of her, even as she finally agreed to marry him.

But one day the man told her an awful secret. He thought he might be gay. And, in fact, he had been messing around with men for two years. The girl was devastated.

But it was like this beast got unleashed. Her sexuality, so long primed and fertile, was finally able to come out into the sun [bad, bad analogy, but whatever....]. On only the third night after her breakup, she met some guy in a bar, got drunk, and made out with him. But she felt nothing. It was like kissing wood.

However, she ran into this man again a couple of nights later. This time, she wasn't so drunk, and she could see how sexy he was, and her long-buried sexuality stirred. There was nothing to recommend this man except a tight body, feral blue-green eyes, and a way with words. Perfect. She wouldn't get attached.

She started up a sexual relationship with this man. It was just what she needed. He made no demands on her emotionally, and she none on him. They were hot and heavy for about six weeks. But she realized in the meantime she wasn't meeting anyone else, because she was with him all the time. Meanwhile, he had an ex-girlfriend he was sleeping with, and sometimes the ex took priority. That bugged her. Eventually, she told the man they shouldn't see each other anymore.

Meanwhile, she was at a party one night. There was a lot of tall, dark, hot foreign men there. Any one of them would be perfect for a sexual fling. She started off many conversations that night, but nothing really gelled. She was getting ready to leave and thought she'd hit the bathroom. A man in front of her turned around and began flirting with her. From what she could tell in the dark, he was very cute. But he wasn't the swarthy bad boy type she had been on the hunt for. Nevertheless, she decided to have a drink with him, and because she was still in such a slutty mindset, she began kissing him right away.

The man emailed her the next morning and asked for a date. This kind of scared her. He was probably the good guy type who wanted something serious right away. She agreed to a date, but she'd have to set him straight.

They went out and to her surprise, she was still attracted to him. The man talked her up into his apartment, and she went all out to impress upon him what a slutty girl she was and how she was just looking for sex. She felt kind of bad about that, because he seemed like such a sweet, wholesome guy. But she'd been with a sweet, wholesome guy for 10 years, and he turned out to be a complete stranger. So she was scared of that type.

But the guy, let's call him Joe, turned out to be not so sweet and wholesome after all. Eventually, they began teasing each other with tales of their sexual derring-do. The badder he seemed, the more she liked him. She also began to see a highly sexual side of Joe. The sweet, wholesome guy she thought he was at the beginning had virtually disappeared. But she knew she wouldn't get emotionally attached to him, because he had some very odd personality traits, and they had virtually nothing in common. Perfect.

Somehow, over the course of their relationship, they began emailing every day. His writing kept her intrigued and interested. But still, things were strange. He would pursue her relentlessly, seem to get mortally jealous if she flirted with anyone else, even invited her back to meet his family in his home country, but at the same time seemed to have no interest in dating her for real. But what did it matter? She wasn't looking for a boyfriend. She'd had that for ten years, and it had gotten deadly dull.

But one day, the girl went on a date with a man she'd met a couple of months previously. She really liked this man, let's call him Muhammed. He was everything Joe was not. He was fun, he was highly sexual and verbal, he liked the same movies and music she did. This was a guy she could get attached to, and that scared her. But she thought she'd give it a shot.

Much to her annoyance, the date with Muhammed went well, and they ended up in bed as usual, but she felt it was all kind of mechanical. She wasn't really into it. She wracked her brain to figure out what was going on. She didn't feel this way when she was with Joe. Dammit.

She tried to tell Joe about this in a couple of their email exchanges, but he would just ignore the topic. He even pretended he didn't receive a long email she had written about it, explaining her confusion, and whether or not they should even keep seeing each other. They have a strange relationship, which she values enormously, and one that seems to work on many levels despite all the odds, but she began to realize it was only a matter of time before she got shunted aside for someone else.

She thought she could rectify the situation by going on as many dates as humanly possible. She went on a date with a handsome 43-year-old man who seduced her. But again, after she left his apartment, she drunk-dialed Joe. She was clearly losing her mind.

Meanwhile, Joe was dating up a storm, and seemed to have fallen for a girl who was the opposite of what she had become. A good girl, who helped out cancer patients. She figured Joe would tire of her eventually, but the girl cut it off with Joe, and now she wondered if that would only inflame Joe's interest. Damn do-gooders!

She made a date with a fireman so hot he could be on one of those fireman's hunks calendars they put out every year. She hoped like hell she wouldn't think about Joe while she was on her date with him.

She's a confused girl. But she's a good girl, and a bad girl, all wrapped into one. And she figures she'll get out of this mess somehow.

THE END

ARE YOU SAD?

You should
know...

that still my life

is consumed

by you...

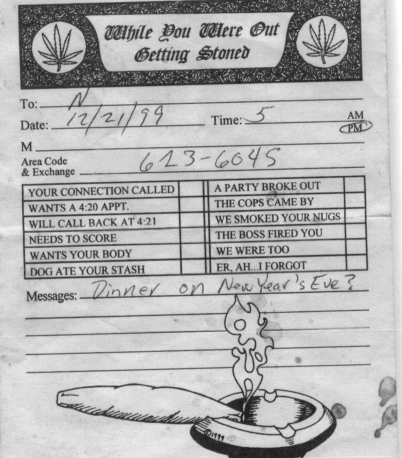

While You Were Out Getting Stoned

To: N

Date: 12/21/99   Time: 5   AM **PM**

M

Area Code & Exchange: 613-6045

YOUR CONNECTION CALLED		A PARTY BROKE OUT	
WANTS A 4:20 APPT.		THE COPS CAME BY	
WILL CALL BACK AT 4:21		WE SMOKED YOUR NUGS	
NEEDS TO SCORE		THE BOSS FIRED YOU	
WANTS YOUR BODY		WE WERE TOO	
DOG ATE YOUR STASH		ER, AH...I FORGOT	

Messages: Dinner on New Year's Eve?

printed on recycled paper

Darling, I've been meaning to ask you this for a long time. How about a photograph of you? There is a spot on my desk drawer that my eye catches the first thing in the morning and the last thing at night and I can't think of nothing I'd like better than to have your picture there —

Hey,
I am sorry for making
you feel bad. I will talk
to you later. bye

Nick

Rosie

Ten minutes after our conversation yesterday, I found myself face to face with a six-foot tall plastic pig. He was dressed in an apron, wearing a chef's hat, had his hoof on his hip and was smiling seductively. Restaurant supply, I have found, is the most reliable place to start ant search. But it occurred to me that before I commit a felony, get arrested or have to spend the better half of a day in jail for defacing public property outside Working Class, I should at least take you out to dinner, 'a last meal' if you will. You're wonderfully interesting; you talk a lot but that's all right because your smile is worth it. Besides being beautiful, I like your name.

Barnaby

Dear Daniel,
Thank you for a great week - You brought back a smile in me that doesn't surface all that much. Although the choice I made this week may not have been a totally wise choice, I don't regret it and I'm so glad I got the to meet you + know you + smooch you too.
I wanted you to know that your conversation stimulated me, your intellect impressed me, your body amazed me and your smile melted me.
The first thing Theo said to me was that I looked different - And he was right - I feel different
You've opened up a side of me that I wasn't really sure I wanted to see - but here it is and I'm dealin' with it.

- I have to go now - but thanks again for such a great time
               XOXO D.

PLEASE DELIVER

Shakawa Lodge Game Reserve
FAX # 27 15 575 1027
One Page

miss

Feel or suffer from the lack of; *"he misses his girlfriend"* 2: fail to attend an event or activity; *"he missed his plane"* [ant: attend] 3: fail to reach or get to 4: be without. [syn: lack] [ant: have]

you

Used to refer to the one or ones being addressed; *"I'll lend you the book. You shouldn't work so hard"* 2: used to refer to an indefinitely specified person; one *"You can't win them all"*

madly

adv 1: in a desperate manner; *"he misses her madly"* 2: in an insane manner; *"he behaved insanely"; "he behaves crazily when he is off his medication"* syn: insanely, crazily, dementedly] [ant: sanely] 3: (used as intensives) extremely; *"he was madly in love"*

I do – and hope that you are having a wonderful time. All is well (and beautiful) back home.

July 22, 2001

Today I watched a
leaf fall.
I saw it float around
until it landed into a
pile of leaves.
Other people passed by but took no
notice of the leaf.
They thought it was ordinary.
When I looked at the leaf, know what
I saw?

Beauty.

(The leaf)

(It was pretty)

12/24/2003

IT'S HARD TO BELIEVE THAT
ONE YEAR AGO I NEVER
DREAMED OF THE REAL
POSSIBILITY OF US ACTUALLY
BEING TOGETHER. I LOVE YOU
SO MUCH. WHEN I THINK OF
ALL THE EVENTS, EMOTIONS
AND TRIALS THAT WE HAVE
BEEN THROUGH OVER THE LAST
YEAR, IT OVERWHELMS ME.
STILL, THE CONSTANT THOUGHT
AND DESIRE OF SHARING OUR
LIVES TOGETHER HAS NEVER
WANED. I DO KNOW THAT WE
ARE PERFECT FOR EACH OTHER,
AND IN SOME WAY GOD DID
MEAN FOR US TO BE TOGETHER.
IT'S SO UNFORTUNATE THAT

POSSIBLY HIS ORIGINAL PLAN
WAS THWARTED BY YOUR
MOTHER'S DESIRE TO CONTROL
YOUR YOUNG ADULT LIFE.
ALSO, THAT THE LIVES OF OUR
FAMILIES HAS BEEN TURNED
UPSIDE DOWN. STILL, GOD IS
ABLE TO MAKE GOOD OUT OF
THE MOST HURTFUL TIMES
AS YOU WELL KNOW, I
KNOW AS WE CONTINUE TO
PRAY FOR HEALING, HE WILL
DO THAT IN THE HEARTS OF
ALL THOSE WE LOVE. THANK
YOU FOR GIVING UP YOUR
WORLD TO COME BE A PART
OF MY WORLD — ONE THAT
WE CAN SHARE EACH DAY
BY EXPRESSING IT IN WAYS
THAT WE BOTH NEVER THOUGHT
WE COULD EXPERIENCE —
I LOVE YOU — MERRY CHRISTMAS

So, you wanna know what I want? I want it all. I want to be in love so much it hurts. The frissons. The pin pricks. The mind-blowing sex. The connection. And I want to be married with kids I adore and a husband who makes me feel safe, sexy, smart, secure, silly, serious, salacious, sinful, serene, satisfied. I want someone who makes me laugh until milk comes out my nose (only I don't drink milk). I want to finish someone's sentences. I want to believe in someone, in something, in a future that's not just about laundry and soccer practice and subdivisions and minivans and guilt-tripping grandparents. I want to make someone a better person. I want to be a good example. I want to love some kids into the world. I want someone who stimulates my brain as much as my body. I want to taste everything and go everywhere. I want to give and I want to get. I want too much and I want it all in one person.

So, what do I want from you? That's hard to say because it's not really about want, it's about wish. Do I wish you were that person for me? Yes. Do I wish that you weren't married with kids and that I wasn't living with someone and that even though we work together we could explore the possibilities and that all my dreams would come true? Duh. But you are, and I am, and we can't and they won't. So the question is, do I want just a little, or I should say, a little more? Sure, all the time I do. But I know a little's not going to be enough and then I'll want more. And then maybe I won't want more, but you will. Or you won't and I will. And then there will be nothing and I don't want that at all.

February 2, 1969

February 2, 1969

—

February 2, 1970

A Year With

POOKS & DUDE

Familiar Faces & Phrases.

The top ten phrases
for this past year:

Five, please, just five, I promise.
I hold you completely responsible.
The first year is the hardest.
Nice.
Ver nice.

You fucking bitch, who the hell
do you think you are?

Who *do* you love?
I'm so tired, please, five?
I love Dude.
I love Pooks!

Happy Anniversary - Feb. 2, 1978

A bit of a hassle moving to

1 Chauncy Street
Apartment 15
Cambridge, Mass. 02139

But we made it -
with a little help from
our friends.

Look, quickly, black bra + panties.
Nothing else.
Shit, they closed the curtain.

Please, call Mr. Chasin. I hate
the floor.

We have more
nic-nacs than anyone
in the world.

We have such a nice
house.
Just like big people.

> Sent: Monday, April 25, 2005 10:46 PM
> Subject: RE: Hey
>
> Hello ▓▓▓▓ to be the most sincere and open, the whole thing summarizes in
> one simple sentence: I don't want to hurt you anymore. You have been such an
> excellent, nice and sweet person to me and I have not treated you the way
> you deserve to be treated. It is not if I miss you or not, or how I perceive
> you. It is that I feel embarrassed to even talk to you. I don't know why I
> can't just be nice and honest with you. Well, I am honest, but it is that we>
> just don't seem to get on the same page.
>
> You and I enjoy each others company and intimacy, but I don't see myself
> falling in love with you. I wish I could explain. I wish I could keep you as
> my friend but I know you wouldn't accept that.
>
> I did horrible things to you and I feel terribly sorry about it. I hope you
> believe me. And I don't know what part of the difference I see in you is a
> consequence of what I have done. Maybe I just didn't want to see how you
> were and now I do. I don't know.
>
> My last couple of days have been complicated from many aspects: work,
> personal, friends and family. I would need pages and pages of emails to tell
> you everything. I have felt weak for the first time in a long time and I am
> questioning some of the decisions I have made in my life. Believe me or not,
> after all the secure things I have now (job, house, etc.), I feel that I
> don't know where I am heading.
>
> You are the only person that knows this now. I don't want to tell anybody
> about it. It is like the foundation of what I am is damaged and I don't know
> how to repair it.
>
> This email started one way and ended up completely different. Sorry.
>
> I am going through rough times right now and I don't know what to do.
> My mom is coming in 3 weeks and I wish I can open up to her and tell her all
> these things.
>
> I hope I made sense here tonight. Sorry I didn't address the main topic. I
> know this is selfish to ask, but keep praying for me because it looks like I
> am not praying enough
>
> Bye
>
>

☺ **Happy events will take place shortly in your home.** ☺

6/20/97

Jerry —

Roses are red, Violets are blue,
I hope you enjoyed your birthday,
going to see U2!

HA! I made a silly rhyme!
Look at what my fortune cookie
said yesterday. What do you think
that could be?

Roz

Sweet Pirate
hours alone,
staining your
what voyage d
Where will th
carry you? My
my spoils--yo
Ravage me wit
drenched mout
carpenter han

assing the
anding and
ship. For
you prepare?
currents
port is open,
s. Come.
your wine
and
s.
      Your princess east

Dear Leslie;   4·15·03

It's a dusty one today. Our tent has no floor, so the
dust is everywhere. At least the wind is keeping the heat
down.

They say we should be moving even further north; probably
by the time you get this. But it seems the farther away
you get, the better and faster the support comes, since they're
almost forced to fly it in on C130's.

I guess it's green and cooler there, so if we have to spend
the summer here, it'll be tolerable. I'm of course hoping they
just let all of us come home, and let some other country
handle the occupation crap.

I have a feeling there'll be alot of idle time, just waiting
to get the hell out of here.

They gave us some bottled water today, so I get a break from
the chlorine! I'm going to save all the lemon aid for the
"hard times". Keep sending that stuff! Water is truly like gold
out here. Nothing else matters if you don't have that.

By the time you read this, I'm sure your birthday has
come and gone, and maybe even our 22nd.

I just want you to know how much I love you, and
how much you matter to me. I've got your picture
in front of my ID card in my wallet, so every time I pull it
out, I see your smiling face, and beautiful eyes.
So I hope your birthday was wonderful, and that the kids
made you a cake!

I miss you like a cool breeze, and the muddy smell of
a new spring complete with flowers, and green grass.

Love,
   Gregory ☺

What I Want

Tonight, there are two things I want.

The first thing I want is a park bench.
Wooden, weathered, solid, comfortable.
And with a view. Doesn't have to be of the
ocean. Could be a simple garden.
Or a squirrel in a tree.
Would you sit next to me, on my park bench?
Would you take my hand and help me
watch that squirrel?

The last thing I want tonight: you.
You and me. You, me, and an entire day
for us to spend together,
any way we choose.

2/26/98

Anna,

   I figured there had to be
something 'auspicious' about your
first birthday as my wife, but
I couldn't quite figure it out.

That is, until I thought about how
for every birthday of yours hereafter,
I will be next to you celebrating
it — as we grow older together in love.

Yours,
Avnish

gold-by Donald Hall POSTC

QUELISTS

Pale gold of the walls, gold
of the center of daisies, yellow roses
pressing from a clear bowl. All day
we lay on the bed, my hand
stroking the deep
gold of your thighs and your back.
We slept and woke
entering the golden room together,
lay down in it breathing
quickly, then
slowly again,
caressing and dozing, your hand sleepily
touching my hair now.

We made in those days
tiny identical rooms inside our bodies
which the men who uncover our graves
will find in a thousand years,
shining and whole.

I love you!
(more + more every day)

Bozeman MT
59715

Hello♥ I'm bored. I had nothing better to do. I'm gonna be at Tom's house, and then go to the game. I hope you can come.

(Here goes nothing) will you go out with me? I know you'll say "No", and you probably won't talk to me, plus U like.....(of course U know). I'll be at Tom's so call me there. (— 3950). If you say "No" (which will happen), can we still be friend.
DON'T TELL EMILY SHE WAS RIGHT!

See Ya.
Sobo

P.S. If you say "Yes" (It won't happen), we better ralk to eachother more, than U and Kraft.

OK. I have humiliated myself with McLawyer. We went to the movies Saturday night. I decided if that ▬▬could get him drunk and make out with him so could I. Well, I bought Jack Daniels and Crown Royal miniatures and put them in my purse then handed them to him in the movie. I felt all warm and fuzzy, but it did nothing for him. Evidently, Crown Royal and Coke is a better aphrodisiac than chocolate for me because I just wanted to make out with someone. Unfortunately, despite all my leaning over on his armrest in the movie and trying to drape myself seductively against the side of my car in hopes that he would get a clue didn't work. All I got was a side hug. I have been demoted to the side hug. I was up to the frontal hug. Anyway, last night we were talking about how we still had the Jack Daniels left for our movie cokes. I said I would not be drinking any more dark liquor because I felt loopy and wanted to make out with someone. I also proceeded to tell him that he was lucky I let him make it out of the parking lot. He was like "You wanted to make out with me?" I said yeah and he was like " Sorry I was such a putz." Well, now he knows I could jump him and I will probably never hear from him again. Actually, I have his mattress and bed in my parent's basement. Maybe I should hold them hostage. What do you think?

Leigh

I wish I was here.

Love
Paul

Hope your feeling better

Take it easy tonight. I'll give

you a call from work to tell

you my plans. I've got a

Surprise for you tommorow.

I wont tell you what it is

So don't try to get it out of

me. Got to get to work so Bye

I love you with all my heart ♡

Jerry

Look! I made the bed! →

In writing anything to you, I always end up frustrated with the results. One reason for that is because I don't like my writing (or pretty much anything else about myself for that matter), and the other reason is a lot more complicated. I could sit here and write an entire novel about my love for you but it would never be able to fully express how I feel. Describing my love for you is like trying to explain why snow is white. They are both unchangable facts of life that cannot be argued. I have a hard time remembering if there was ever a time I didn't love you. And you know what, maybe I always did love you, even before we met. I was always in search of someone like you. Someone that would always love me and not be afraid to tell me that she loved me. Someone who would touch me with soft tenderness that showed to me just how much she loved me. Someone that I could say anything to, and who I actually truly enjoyed talking to. Someone that would make a wonderful, nice, caring, loving mother. I love you and if you ever want to be reminded of that, just look in my eyes. They will always show my love for you... even when you pick at your fingers. :)

Yours Forever,

This Floating Life

still floating

11.25.2005

Birthday Letter

Dear Ben,

I can't call you on your birthday so I have to write. Wherever you are now, I'm sure you're surfing the Web if at all possible.

I think about you all the time. I try to picture your face. Often we would be driving somewhere and I would turn and study the side of your face. You would wear that heavy grey polar fleece pullover and orange TiVo cap. You had a cute long nose and those rectangular glasses. I liked when your hair was longer and curling a little. You were getting a few silver hairs at your temples. I tried to picture what you would look like as you got more grey.

I try to remember our conversations. You would bring me up to speed on your friends and family -- their comings and goings -- and show me your old home movies. I already felt as if I knew everyone. Or at least, I knew their bar mitzvahs. You made that movie of your cat while you were home on break from college because you were pretty certain that was the last time you were going to see him. That was one long movie. You followed him around the yard when he wasn't doing very much, just loafing and poking around. And that turned out to be the last time you saw him.

Many people have noted with regret that we have so few photos and movies of you. You took reams of photos and hours of video, but you always were behind the camera. I don't even have a picture of the two of us. Everything that happened between us, with a few exceptions, was just us -- and now I'm carrying it alone. I have to talk/write/rant about you just to help bear it, even though I know you would be terribly embarrassed. But you knew what you were getting into with me. You read the whole blog before we even met.

You could dish pretty well yourself, though. When we first met you boasted about your colorful stories, and I remember a lot of them now. Generally your full-blown stories about people would fall into two categories -- People who Made Good Decisions and People who Made Bad Decisions. People who made good decisions, such as being the first to move to a particular up-and-coming town, often had been recipients of your advice. People who made bad decisions often had ignored advice from you -- buying a substandard appliance, for example -- and were punished with some kind of trouble, such as a defective unit, as a result.

Either way, you gave a lot of advice. When I was mad at you I theorized you saw everyone as projects that needed your improvements, and that you mostly related to people by criticizing them. In calmer moments I realized that you didn't criticize to be mean. You were just ridiculously informed about an insane number of things and were trying to help people out, freely dispensing your opinion whether it was welcome or not. And whatever it was, usually you were right.

I don't think I ever saw you mean. You could be smug; frosty; imperious; gracious; tender; passionate. But not mean.

I still haven't renovated my kitchen, but I'm holding on to the sketch you made. You sent it to me the first week we were dating. In my book, that's a no-money-back-you're-getting-laid guarantee.

You tried to give me music advice once. What a disaster. I had been having difficult gigs and you were videotaping them all. The night you tried to play a show back to me and make running commentary -- like "why don't you smile more at the audience?" -- I almost knocked your block off. It was the only time I told you to go fuck yourself and really meant it. But you seemed to like it when I got sassy.

You continued to try to be helpful. We even tried an album cover shoot in Central Park, scouting around to find the spot where Nina Simone sat for the cover of her first record. We climbed giant, icy "keep off" rocks and froze our asses sitting on them to get a good shot of me with the pond and bridge behind. Days later, you produced another pearl: "I think your record cover should be . . . the outline of your naked body." Good grief, Ben.

Last year on your birthday we met up at Columbus Circle. Your instructions from me were to wear a suit that fit. I spotted you from across the plaza -- you looked so tall and handsome in your suit and trenchcoat. You were taller than everybody. It was not too cold; holiday lights were up; the Salvation Army lady was there with her bell and kettle. When we kissed hello I felt so nervous.

Between our fancy dinner and jazz at Lincoln Center, we strolled through Borders in the Time Warner Center -- you pointed out Weird N.J. magazine. Why do I keep remembering that now? We spent the rest of the weekend watching Lord of the Rings and debauching. Afterward, you didn't call me for days. God I was furious -- but that did result in our setting up a schedule. And that worked.

I remember your signature touches. You would bring tea and cookies to me on the couch and plop your legs in my lap. Self-righteously, like a huge cat. As we rode the bus in the morning, you would plant your hand on my knee and squeeze. You would TiVo stuff for us to watch together. Weeknights were nice and slow with you. It shocks me now to realize how much of a steady presence you were.

Sometimes I get hysterical wondering where the hell you've disappeared to. I force myself to remember the night on the pier, as you were losing strength, and then later as your soul left your body. I tell myself this was the end of the story. Of course, that's impossible. Your story is carried on by everyone who cared about you. Ed wrote a beautiful remembrance of you.

It's really cold tonight so I'm pulling out your down comforter. Saro threw up on the green blanky and I need something warm.

I miss you, Ben. You are never far from my thoughts. Now go fuck yourself.

Love, Erica

posted by Erica @ 11:27 PM   3 comments   links to this post

3 Comments:

Stay warm for me and
have a nice day. You are my
sweetheart ever with popsicle feet

Love you

Measurement

10/05/06 12:57

Text: ※□□□□Small→H

Forward

dear mike   august 1 2001

i dreamt about passing over this
bridge so many times. this is
where we determined our midpoint
to be, the ambassadorbridge. one
mileof metal separating detroit
from windsor. i would stand on c
one end, you on the other, and we
would meet halfway. i'd touch
          your face, and it wouldn't
          seem so foreign. features
     so familiar eventhough so
muchtime had passed. but then th
the tears would come back with a
all inthe memories. the good one

ones and the bad would drown us
both, and we would begin to sink
in ixx lake ontario. the lake
knew something we didn't. is it
the right time for us to inmeet
xxi again? i want you back in
my life so bad. part of me is
          fighting for that. the othe
          other part is struggling
     in the past trying to forget
but wanting to remember the
first time. in detroit. i xxx
t ouched your fac e.

dear mike...   december 2002

i miss you in the morning,
     (laying on your tummy with hands as pillows).
          xkxixnemexixwkmexymexxmx
i miss that moment when your eyes first open,
     (a slow smile comes across your glassesless
                                        face).

i miss your touch,
          your kiss
               your smell.

i miss riding bikes with you,
     (we would xtry to ride side-by-side holding k
                                        hands).

i miss the way you dance,
     (even if it did embarrass me at times).

i miss talking to you on the phone,
     (when it was for hours, just before bed
          and i would smmetimes fall asleep to your
                         voice).

i miss listening to the first bonny 'prince'billy record
               together,
     (you always made me smile when you'd dance around
               and do sign lanuage to the first song
               side a).

i miss the way we would lay together,
     (your head using my stomach as a pillow).

i miss waiting for you,
     (frantic for your e-mails,
          going out of the way to see if you had written).

i miss your quite strumms on the guitar,
     (your voise softly singing to me).

          i miss your arms around me.

there is so much more i miss. i could write pages of things.
part of me wonders if i miss you so much because thats
how i spent most of our relationship: missing you.
we were apart more than we wexx were ever together; there was
detroit and our two days; i went up to ottawa for a week;
you came down to chicago for a week. then you got duel
citizenship and lived with me in chicago for four months.
it's so funny to me when i look back, maybe we could only
love each other from a distance.

dear mike ᵡᵡ   march 24th 2003, monday

everyday my thoughts come back ᵡto you. i see
a sweater you'd likeᵡᵢ. i listen to the new
smog record and wonder if you are too. did ᵡᴍ
you know that i've never koved anyone as much
as you? (and that i stillᴍ ᵡcan't get past
you) you left me with such uncertainty. three
years ago you turned away from me at the grey
hound station. i didn't want you to leave. i
wanted to touch you one more time, whether to
hit you or hug you. everything had happenedᵡᵡ
so quickly; the cheating, the break up, the
leaving. all i've ever wanted was a better e
explaination. you still wanted me to move to
montreal with you. you wanted to be with me
but not with me. you still loved me but as a
friend. you ᴍ just wanted a break from relationships. but then, why would you kiss herᵡᵢᵡ
the second i was on that plane to new york?
why did you move back to ottawa and start to
date someone as soon as you got there? all ᵢ
i've ever wanted was the truth from you, i
hate being left with so many questions.

      this is the last time i'll say
            goodbye.
            rebecca

path to secret campground (behind Nor...) when other way is...

go straight past weird buildings
follow on left of river or
follow signs to Stables.

I'm pretty sure you can
take this path too.

Valet Parking

gravel ←

gate w/ Don enter → par...

water

pretty big deciduous tree

cut uphill just before water.

walk on loose rocks until you see a huge rock on right cut around until you hit water walk IN the wat... you hit the D... water comes casca... the Royal Arches on rocks. Not t... comfortab... P...

It gets pretty hot. You should probably bring a watermellon.

huge rock

hot rocks for naked people

shade for reading

✱

↓ Royal Arches

Parking

Frog Pond

THE LITTLE KNOWN DIRECTIONS TO A COOL SPOT FOR PEOPLE WHO HATE CLOTHES

Car-Road

Foot path

weird → gate thing to hotel

footpath

. Alot of rattlesnakes here. Don't tell J.E.M. about them or he'll never go (Just go first)

...til

S HOT-TUB

Down from

d heats up

t but definately

Jet a very large

out definately large

ough for a little seduction.

Another juicy fact: Across the street from the Housekeeping Camp Shuttle Stop is a rope-swing.

* only give this info out to important people

d,
your emoticon

doesn't make me feel like this:

```
  —    —

  O    O

     #

  — — — —
```

or like this:

```
  —    —

  0    0

     ^

  — — —
  —    —
```

it makes me feel like this:

```
  —    —

  *    *

     ~

 —        —
 —        —
  — — — —
```

just like that.
-m

Here's a special card
that's bringing
At this special time of year
Very special,
happy greetings
To somebody mighty dear

Well, listen sweetie. I do need to really chill out on this. The 50 emails a day is distracting to the point where I'm getting barely any work done. I have a TV project that I am in charge of, with extremely tight deadlines, a complicated story due, and I have completely ignored planning for India. I love our twisted exchanges, but I think the cons have begun to outweigh the pros. It does not seem that this relationship is made for anything other than what it is, and we have pretty much plumbed the depths of it.

I am open to doing something with you occasionally (yes, you will have to ask; yes, you will have to give me notice) if you like, but I simply cannot continue with the long drawn-out email exchanges. Basically, I need to get my life back.

I thank you for spending as much time with me as you did; it came at a time in my life when I really needed a distraction, and you certainly provided one. Except for your insanity, you are one of the coolest/funniest people I know. And I really did develop genuine feelings of friendship, and dare I say it, some degree of romantic attachment to you. But it def. cannot continue on this way, making me even crazier than I already am.

Take care and we'll catch up in the future, I'm certain. :)

Better idea.

Happy Mother's Day, Honey

To my incredibly <u>sexy</u> wife,

You don't actually have to share the bath, as the picture shows, but since I know you're in desperate need of some relaxation (and getting into the bath isn't your idea of the most hygenic way to do it), this card comes complete with a promise from me to clean both our bathrooms thoroughly — including scrubbing the tubs.

Love, Charles

PETER J. DOUGHERTY,
CHIEF OF POLICE.

PALMERTON, PA. Dec. 22d 1911

My dearest Lizzie;—

I dont know whether you seen me this morning or not, I saw you by the drug store where you met Miss Weignant. I expect to go to bed this afternoon, So I must write to my Sweetheart first.

I just received three nice presents from the Muellers, I appreciate them very much as I did yours, Tomorrow I will give you your ring, I received it yesterday and had the jewelers wife take it to Allentown and have it engraved. So I will be there to put it on your finger tomorrow afternoon, I showed it to the folks here and they think it very pretty, Sallie said if I would give it to her she would be my wife. But Peter's love is all for his dear Lizzie, and hopes to make her happy when he gives it to her.

Well dearest, I told my mother of our en-
gagement, My sister had heard it in Palmerton Wednesday
when she visited the hospital, She hadn't told my
mother, So I had to break the news. Now they
all know it.

When I said I felt different I didn't mean that
I felt badly about it, I feel happier than ever
I don't know just how the weather is going to
be tomorrow, If it is like this it would be as well
for you to take the 342 on the C.R.R. and go
right through arriving at Reading 545. Then
we could spend the afternoon at Lamoreux's.
We can decide that tomorrow, Then I will
not see my sweetheart for some time.
But my heart goes with her and my love
will last no matter how long we are apart.

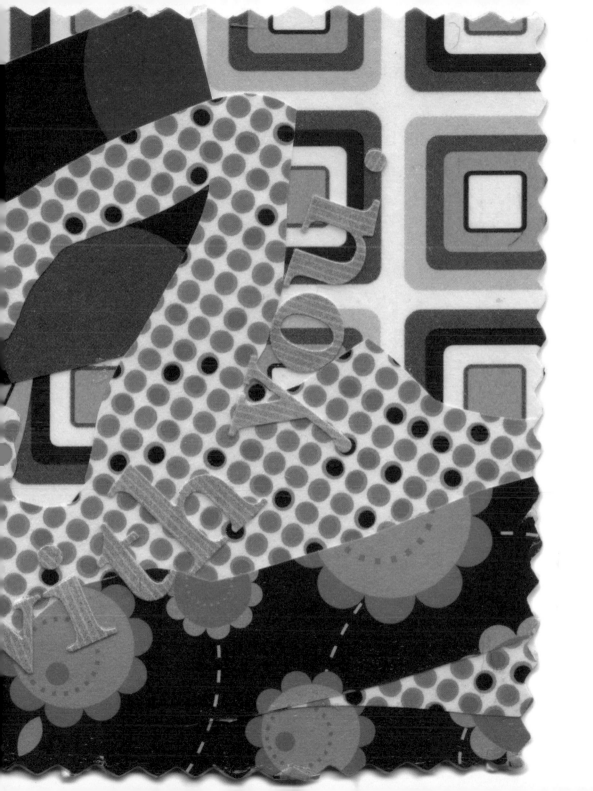

I dreamt about you last night

I was at camp
With strangers
In a room full of pianos
Oskar Eustis was teaching us how to play piano
By instinct
Without learning the notes

I was pretty good at it

Then I had a class called
Imagining Water
And I floated in the air for a while

I was pretty good at that too

Then you showed up
With your French backpack
And your gold hair
And the hills around us blushed so green

I had not noticed them before

You let me lift your shirt a little
And kiss your stomach
And it was warm and soft like perfect bread
And it made me hungry

And even in the dream
I felt that quiet buzz of rightness
That happens when you're around

have produced something
so amazing.
    From the first moment
Sean arrived you were the
dedicated and caring father.
I only hope Sean will be able
to tell you one day himself how
much he appreciates your love.
    Happy First father's Day,
        my love —
            Love always,
            me XXXX
                OOOO

I look into your eyes

and find my soul mate.

I hear your voice

and never feel alone.

Beside you, I believe

in love unending

and feel the deepest joy

I've ever known.

WISHING YOU A WONDERFUL
FATHER'S DAY

Thank you for the amazing
gifts you have brought into my
life — your love and our
beautiful son. It is such a
precious moment when I
look at the two of you together
and marvel at how we could ←

I know that dollar-wise things have been
a little tight, and looking back a little
unfair, too. You know that eventually things
are going to ease up a bit, and in the
mean-time, I promise to make it more
fair. The whole situation is unfair to you.
You shouldn't have to sacrifice like this,
but you have done so willingly and cheerfully.
I really appreciate it! You're a champ.
I'm doing ~~everything~~ I can to make
~~life more~~ our evenings together, longer. I
hope you'll be patient until, one way
or another I start getting home earlier.
I thank you for all you've done
for us, endured for us, and loved for
us. My marriage is so important to me -
because of whom I married. You've made me
the happiest, most happiest, of all happy.

Love,

Natie-pooh
a.k.a. Nate the "Nate"

Sent: Tuesday, May 16, 2006 9:36 PM
Subject: hey

I missed you the second you left my office today. I'm so excited about our first house & I'm SO excited about our first night there together! I can't wait to start house projects! We will have so much together! I love you & am lucky I'm marrying you!

i bought

whipped cream.

What we danced

through in ██████, on the Cape, and last week, was politics, persuasion, lobbying for better ground, and the words spoken seemed sad and desperate. Anyone would get scared playing a pinball machine that tilts on touch. You've worked your magic on me and I've been worked over well, great verbal violence, wit-whipped, smoothed, shaken, loved. I am, and I can't get much more simple than this, afraid of you.

However, we mutually compel mutual attraction. How do I cope with that? I am forever attracted to you, body and mind, inside, outside, with and without. I believe I am more attracted by you than anyone else I've met or hope to meet. But then again, I'm suicidal, at least philosophically. And although I try to resist it, I'm slightly crisis-oriented. And certainly I don't know you. I'll give you that very easily. I don't know you. I only know things about you, the color of your hair, the shape of your shoulders, the pools of brown eye, very seductive. I know temperment. I know some of your expressions. I have a collection of words written by you. You share a few ideas. You use too many adjectives. But I don't know anything about who, exactly, you are, in fact. Which disqualifies me as a participant in many areas of your life, not the least of which is professional counsel. But I'm disqualified in a lot of things—life, the persuit of happiness, wisdom, intellect, culture, politics (I lost twice in two consecutive bids for president of my high school class). In other words, must I know you?

I don't know as much as I want to know. And I know more than I want to. I need and don't need you, etc. and so on. My brain is in shreds, my life is at the very least curiously unsatisfying, if not lonely, and I often fantisize about who or what will fill it, and when and how.

more on the other side

Your letter was read and immediately cherished. It doesn't deserve this as response and so don't consider this a response. I want to be close to you, however that closeness chooses to manifest itself. Yours, indeed, in and out of love.

This is what I was trying to say the other night:

i love

you like

A fat kid

loves CAKE

I think you know how
much my life has changed
for the better since I
first met you in the copy room.
You are the most beautiful
person I've ever known and
my affection for you is
boundless. It's going to be
so hard to come to work
without having your beautiful smile
of wonderful laugh to look forward
to. I will miss you like the
night sky misses the sun, but I will forever look forward to a new day
with you

Report Spam   Delete   More actions...   >

oh, Inbox

More options   Aug 16

this is torture, torture, torture.

why is this so hard?? I survived a whole day not talking to you 2 1/2 weeks ago. What happened???

i'm not as nice in the world today. i am scowly. i am trying to be good and not fussy, but frankly, this is less fun.   and i am getting grumpy about the prospect of many, many more days like this ahead.

maybe i'll quit school and go be a jewelry maker. that could probably distract me.

xox me

Reply **Forward**

inma,   062705

  mi amore. my life is
mucho blessed to be togother
with you. you of shimmering soul,
deep heart, tuneful mind, and
yummy body. ode to the good
times we share the true life we
bounce in as mates partners
friends lovers humyns being humyn.
you are in me, a part of me. we
are now and eternity streaming
alive joyous yes thrive... ♥

billy

Date: June 20, 2006 11:05:13 AM EDT
Subject: Re: ever!

i stopped at home and figured id read my email....i cant believe youre
real sometimes (i know you are) i never want to leave you when i have to
and i think about you constantly in some way or the other all day, i
havent gave the finger to anyone driving since i met you...seriously taken
by you all the ways and things that make you who you are, all i want is to
know and enjoy more of you, you really do it for me.

Toledo Ohio.
July 28. 1918.

Mr. H. Goldberg :-
Your letter on hand and
I was certainly surprised
after I got through reading
it. I surely did not expect
to get a letter like that
being that we have seen
each others only once and
then I did not have a
chance to speak with
you alone. I am sure
that our correspondence
did not lead up to that.
I surely don't see how
you expect me to answer
you but being that you

say that you want to
know if there is hopes,
I must say that we
all live on hopes, but
we must see that our
hopes come true. It
would be a bad thing
if we did not have "hope"
with us.

I dont know what you
have heard of my
father's desire but
I am sure that you
would think different

if you knew him.
I surely can't see what
you meant by "answer
as soon as possible".
If there is a chance
for you were you can
get a definate answer
at once and I am keeping
you back why don't wait
but go ahead. There is
a saying "That a bird
caught is worth more
then a bird in the
bush."

Trusting that this letter
reaches you in the best
of health.

Hoping that I answered
as soon as you wanted
I remain as ever,

Frank S.

P.S. The family sends
their best regards.

Give my best regards
to your sister.

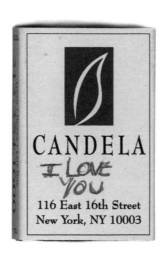

PHoebe
I loVe you And
I MIght marry
you. Jacob

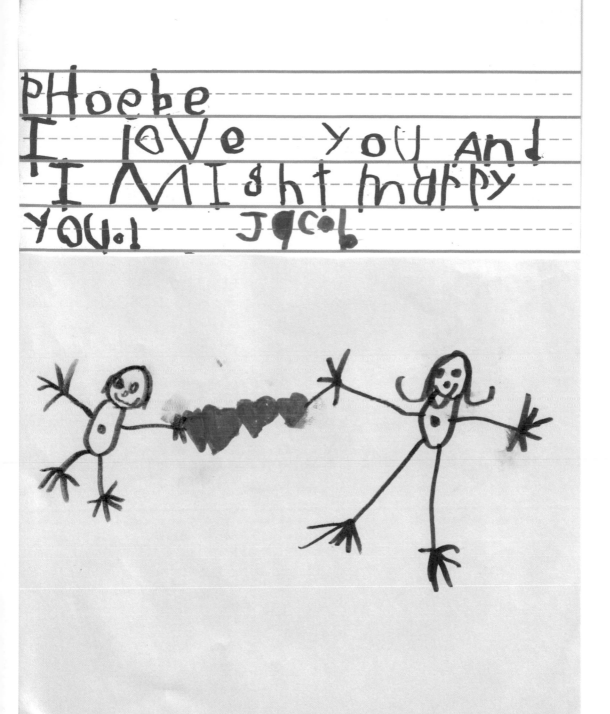

I'm in another hotel tonight.
And I'm thinking of you.
I'm thinking about that time
you tied me down to your bed
and unbuttoned my jeans.
And just used your tongue.

Do you ever feel so sad that your heart hurts? Since the moment i walked into my apartment i cant help but notice every single mark you left behind... not to mention your adidas sweater i am wearing now to smell your smell to feel like you are closer to me. When they said distance makes the heart grow fonder they werent lying... i am once again reminded never to take anything for granted... especially your love, your patience, your presence...

d-

ps: 524160 minutes to go!

Dear Chelsea...

It is New Year's Day. I'm sitting in yet another new apartment in downtown Manhattan. I moved in yesterday and the place looks like a garage sale. The experience of signing a lease and moving in sort of drove home the fact that I'm staying here another year, and I have mixed feelings about that. My job is the main reason I'm staying. The travel website I'm working at is sending me to Malaysia in March to write about it.

Other than a few Sommerset Maugham stories I read years ago, I have never even thought of Malaysia; but I am quickly accepting that for two weeks I will become part of it. I will visit Malacca and Kuala Lumpur. I will walk and sleep in the world's oldest jungle and dive in the Indian Ocean. I will climb a mountain in Borneo and meet people from a tribe who believe the universe was created by an arboreal slug. After it all, after those two short weeks, I will return. I will stay in New York so I can see Malaysia. But I can't think of anything else that grounds me to this place. If it weren't for this prospect of getting paid to travel and write, I could walk away from my life here.

It has been ages since I've seen you. I got your Christmas card, and I loved the little poem inside. You are a thoughtful person. I wish I were as good at keeping in touch as you, but my pattern of correspondence is organized according to impulsivity, which I suppose is better than nothing. Unfortunately, my fiction habit works the same way, and unless I change it I won't get published again anytime soon.

Since I'm sitting here in my cluttered new home, with all the material contents of my life staring at me from boxes, I might as well unpack a thought I've kept from you for as long as I've known you. Perhaps this too is impulsive, but I don't care anymore.

I remember a long time ago, when I first met you, we had a conversation out on the balcony of ~~****~~ University. There was a point during that conversation when the hair on my back stood up, and I started to feel something for you. I was with Sally at the time, and I remember looking at you across the table and in a few silent seconds I saw an entirely different life, one in which it was you I was with instead of her. It was like looking at something beautiful and forbidden, and I was scared. When I got together with Sally, I thought she was the right thing, and I didn't think there could be two right things. So I ended the conversation. I stood up abruptly and walked back into the newsroom and told myself that I should not get too close to you, because the temptation would be too great. Knowing what I know now, I should not have walked away so quickly, and I suppose I did because I needed to know what I know now.

The truth is that I still think about that moment. I have thought about it for five years because it was very clear. I don't even know if you remember it, or if you felt anything, but I'm not getting any younger. I could wonder about this for another five years and you could be married and have children, and even if you did remember that moment, it could be dismissed as some past fancy, if it hasn't been already.

I'm getting tired of wondering about you, Chelsea. It is too easy for me to sit here in New York, feeling like an alien, taking no risks, playing my role halfheartedly, and wondering about you three thousand miles away. I meant that stuff about moving to Seattle, but the real reason was so I could be near you. I didn't know how you felt about me, though, and I didn't know how to breach the subject because it sounded insane. I mean, a guy just doesn't leave a pretty good job in New York and move across the country to follow a hunch he had five years ago, especially if he has no idea how the woman feels. It sounded crazy to me, and I was afraid it would sound even crazier to you. I figured it would scare the hell out of you and I wouldn't get any more of those nice cards and letters. It sounds no less crazy now, and God only knows what you're thinking as you read this, but I believe that in this world it is much crazier to let a feeling like that slip away without exploring it.

So there it is, five years later. A large item I have taken with me everywhere, now unpacked. The only one who knows anything about this is our friend Eric ▓▓▓▓▓. I told him that I felt something for you two years ago and he said he had already seen it in his mind. With all respect to him, though, his opinion doesn't mean jack---only yours does. All I want to know is if you remember that moment, if you were there in that place, if you felt the same thing at the same time, if you ever wonder about it, too?

Happy new year, Chelsea. May it bring you fulfillment, love, and all the things that really matter.

P.S.---And if you only think about me as a friend, then don't worry. I will always be your friend, as long as you don't sleep with any members of my family.

January 21, 1997

Dear Jason,

Wow.

Just read your letter. (I've been out of town for two weeks and had to dig it out of a box teeming with bills and junk mail at the post office.) It's only been a few hours and I am still a little giddy, so please excuse me if I ramble.

My Turn: Of course I had a crush on you all the time we knew each other. (It had to have been at least somewhat obvious.) I always felt very connected to you, as if there was something unspoken that we shared on some level. I always enjoyed our talks at the ████, but the "moment" for me happened when we were sitting on the balcony at the Pub discussing the war in Bosnia. Somewhere amidst all that talk of genocide, rape and pillage, a piece of my heart gave itself to you. But you were with Sally, (who always impressed me), and so I pushed the idea out of my mind. Then, when Sally was gone, you were in New York and I was in Portland — interesting though, that we both had in mind the same reason for you moving to Seattle.

You were very brave and honest to write me that letter. I am so totally impressed. I think that we are very much alike in some basic way that doesn't present itself all that often. (You know, brilliant, savvy, profound.) And yet, you are still in New York and I am still in Portland. So what do we do now?

I would love to see what could happen with us. (Two weeks together and we might never want to see each other again.) But I can't make any promises or guarantees. (Wow, Jason, it's hard to believe that we are talking about this after all these years — Which one of us will get rights to the teleplay?) This does seem a bit out of the blue since the most I've hoped for from you lately is a postcard and I had just about given up on that. But if I've learned anything in the past year, it's that life is peculiar and following your heart it the only way to find yourself anywhere the least bit interesting.

Anyway, I've run out of things to say. Or rather, I'm at a loss for words.

But I do want to go on the record saying that what ever happens between us, now, or soon, or even in five years when I'm married and have those kids, I want us to always always be (at least) good friends. Okay?

Write me back soon.

Yours,

Chelsea.

Chelsea.

P.S. I'm going to have to eviscerate Eric for being so goddamn good at keeping secrets.

First off, I would like to apologize again for the event this summer. I realize I should have said something sooner instead of dropping it on you at the end of a great weekend. I'm sorry. You know it seems I have been in the doghouse since I met you. May be one of these days I will somehow redeem myself.

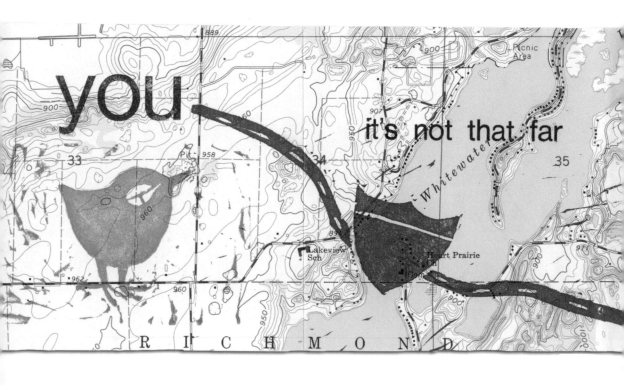

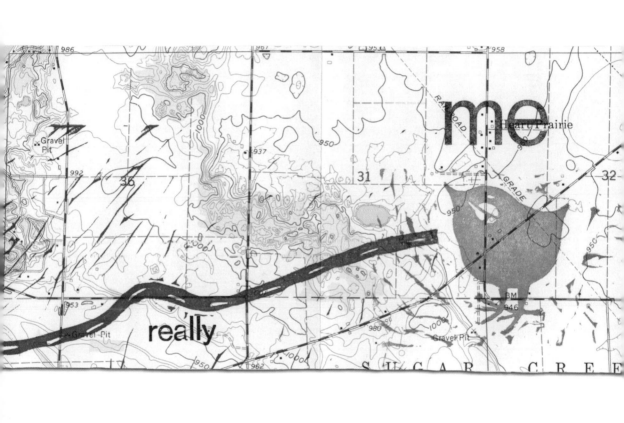

Date: Tue, 20 Jan 2004 15:25:05 -0400
To: Jonathan
Subject: Re: Confession

Sweet Jonathan,

I cried when I read your note, so brave and clear it
pierced my heart. I am honored, awed and deeply moved by
your love--gentle and soft as first snow, fierce and
unshakeable as steel.

Any doubts I had about the authenticity or depth of your
feelings for me are erased by your letter. Even via e-mail
I could see it was signed in blood, from your truest self
to my truest self. I believe every word and I trust that if
I meet you in this place of love, you will do whatever it
takes
To be with me.

It is easy, tempting, to let your feelings for me become my
feelings for you. They are powerful and I am a sponge.
Instead, I need to continue to discover my own feelings for
you and share them as they emerge.

Time together will help me know more, but for today, know
that I miss you.

With a long, long hug,

Monday
February 20th, 1939

Darling:

Thanks so much for your Valentine gift. Your selections
are always in the very best of taste. It really was swell,
darling, and swell of you to send it.

Si, dear, I just know that some day you are going to be
very successful. I don't know why, but somehow I have all
the faith in the world in you. I only wish that I could in
some measure be sharing that "build up" with you. Some people
go through life without having any ambition or ideas, and you
are full of them. Your new idea sounds grand -- much better
than a fox farm or even the Trading Post and camp idea which
was very good. Your idea for having a children's wear store
with a sort of Alice in Wonderland or Mother Goose set-up
is just swell because it is novel, and this seems to be an
age when novel ideas or anything that is just a bit "different"
goes over big. Children's merchandise is always a profitable
business because no matter what, parents won't skimp on their
children. BUT (there always has to be a but) an idea like
this would take an awful lot of capital for it couldn't be
put over in half measures. That is the main drawback. The
idea of having midgets as clerks isn't so very practical.
You might have one or two as a special attraction, and the
regular clerks just petite girls. And then I've always
understood where baby stores made their most profits was
in the department for expectant mothers and that wouldn't
necessarily have to be in miniature. But darling I think
it is a grand idea and I think you are simply marvelous
for being wide-awake enough to think of it. Did you have
anything definite in mind? Let me know what is what, dear.

I really feel very proud that you let me in on your ideas.
Wouldn't it be marvelous if we could be talking them over
instead? *!*

Dear Dan,

It's taken long enough for me to finally get down to writing this to you. I don't want it to be too shallow, nor too melodramatic or sappy. So... here I go. Just bear with me.

I never expected to find some one that meant so much to me in such a short period of time. It feels funny, almost like a belly-ache... and it feels great. This is all so new, but it seems just right, like everything is in its right place.

I haven't had any particular feelings for anyone in such a long time. Now there's all these emotions ~~that~~ coming over me in rushes. I want you to know that if I ever feel the least bit hesitant, I'm just sort of afraid, trying to ~~s~~ sort everything out. I can't believe that something so wonderful is actually so real.

The ~~time I~~ spent with you wasn't just "fun." A word like that doesn't even come close to describing what happened between us. It was all so

natural, so O.K. whenever. I used
to be with anyone it always felt
sort of wrong, almost ~~the~~ dirty. I
never felt that good about it. But
this time it ~~was~~ so raw, so pure.
Everything was perfect. You make
me feel so comfortable with myself,
with my self being with you. You've
brought back the thumping heart-
beat in me - when you feel your chest
is just going to burst open. My breath
heaves just when I look at you,
look into you. That's never happened
to me before. I've never expressed
myself to anyone as I did to you.

I love taking you in in all ways
possible - looking at you, hearing you,
smelling you, tasting you, feeling you.
You are truly an amazing person.

I don't know how to end this. I
refuse to speak of the future. In
my little idealistic world, ~~I~~ everything
stays as it is ~~is~~ right now. And I'm
not sure what words I ~~just~~ should pick
to sum everything up. I just wanted you
to know that I feel very strongly for you.
    Always & ever, Tanya Leigh

The man of your dreams,
perhaps not
maybe just one of the
many that have fallen
but for now I am
ridiculously happy
to be the one who
curls himself around you.

Dear Lindsey,

I am so hating men right now.
Mart dumped me, because I lost my mind and had a weak flashback
moment with Miles. Then I dumped Jim for Aquaman. And then,
Aquaman dumped me for his beach house (not kidding!). He actually
said "I only wish I had met you after the summer." ????? What's
that supposed to mean?!!?????

My feelings are so fucking hurt. I feel it in my arms and legs.
It's like my blood is sad. I feel so stupid for having hope, for
letting myself feel things for him, for calling when he wasn't
calling back. Total humiliation.
I hate feeling so weak and so vulnerable.
I hate that I miss him, that I miss Mart. I hate that I am alone.
I hate that I made him into a superhero he was not. (He dives for
ship wrecks and he has a delicious body, but he is NO aqua man.)
I hate that I bought him jumbo bags of peanut M&Ms because they
were his favorite.
I hate that I want to sleep all the time.
I hate that I even thought for a second about not moving to new
york because
of this.
i hate that i will see him in the gym.
i hate that he doesn't want to kiss me.
i hate that i called mart this morning just to hear his voice,
just to hear
him say he misses me.
i hate that all i want to do is read lame magazines and watch
daytime tv.
i hate that every time i cry over one boy it is like crying over
all of
them again.

HONEY

DE VAIR

DCCCCXVI.

E. B. 896.

Gentiana nivalis.   Small Alpine Gentian.

Reasons Why I Love Kay

I can be myself when I am with you.

Your idea of romance is very simple; dim light and just the two of us.

Because you make me feel like I have never felt before.

I can tell you anything, and you won't be shocked.

Your undying faith in me is what keeps the flame in our love alive.

We're a perfect match, we compliment each other.

Thinking of you fills me with a wonderful feeling.

Your love gives me the feeling that the best is still ahead.

You have never given up on me, even through so many trying times.

You are simply irresistible physically, I love your body.

I love you because you bring the best out of me.

Your terrific sense of humor, you make me laugh.

Every time I look at you, I get such a warm feeling inside.

You're the one who holds the key to my heart.

You always say what I need to hear.

You have taught me the true meaning of love.

You are always in my dreams.

You always tell me what I Love.

Your smile is so genuine.

You cry at happy and sad movies.

You are the most intelligent person I know.

You are so generous.

You always put me before you.

You are always thinking of our health.

You are so funny when you drink "Cosmopolitans"

You live the "4-S" lifestyle.

I love your energy.

You have a passion for life.

Your philosophy is Faith, Family and Friends.

You are passionate about your work.

I love your need to be pampered.

I love your "Dizzy Blondeness".

You are a home body… you love the simple things in life.

You love making love with me.

I love your Heritage.

You Love to laugh

I love it when you sing……especially "Come Out, Come Out"

I love your little sayings such as "Where Was I"

I love your telephone calls.

I love having been in Little Theatre with you.

I love it when you are having fun with friends when I can't be with you.

I love you being Blue Blood…having small wrists and ankles.

I love when you are proud of me.

I love you to love Mr. Lesters.

I love the little surprises you give me.

I love you to like holding my hand and hugging me in public.

I love when you give me the "Breaking News".

I love when you e-mail me interesting sites and articles.

I love when you sing "Say Gentlemen"

I love you great memory.

I love your love for reading.

I love when you use all of your products.

I love that you are an Educator.

I love that you have been widely recognized in your Profession.

I love when you say that I'm a Tedium.

I love your daily e-mails to the family.

I love your poetry.

I love that you are so good to your friends.

I love that you are always Stylish.

You don't get upset when I want to watch sports.

You ask me if I would like to play black-jack at times.

I love your beautiful eyes.

I love how you look at me with those eyes.

I love your thoughtfulness.

I love your tenderness.

I love the way we love so many of the same things.

I love your demand for respect without being controlling.

I love how you would do anything in the world to make me happy.

I love your voice.

I love the way you say "I'm getting ready D".

I love the completeness and oneness I feel when we make love.

I love your sensuality.

I love the way you protect me and defend me.

I love your soft skin.

I love waking up with you at my side.

I love your passion for yoga, skating and walking.

I love the way you inspire me to be more than I am.

I love that we will grow old together.

I love the way you look when you are sleeping.

I love your way with words.

I love that you think I'm smart.

I love that you share everything with me, especially your heart.

I love your strength of character.

I love when we soak together.

I love your little love notes.

I love the way you take care of me.

I love that you can "Raw and Steam"

I love your confidence.

I love that you depend on me.

I love how you love our children.

I love that you want to be with me.

I love our "Dates Together"

I love that you've learned how to scratch my back.

I love that you call me "D".

I love when you ask me to sing "Put Your Head on My Shoulder"

I love your Honesty.

I love you when you write on me with your finger.

I love when you tell me I'm handsome.

I love that you love me.

Dear Eva—

My mom asked me if we were going to get married someday and she thought you were wonderful and would go far in life

Love, Terry

P.S. I think you're wonderful too?

I ♥ like to watch you work because your assertiveness turns me on—

I had a fabulous night and I'm looking forward to many more

Love, Terry

P.S. I'm glad to be the only man ~~woman~~ in your life again

I WANT YOU
SO BAD

I think I enjoy being single. I was very lonely for a long time after we went separate ways. I missed the emotional pulls and pushes, the physical caresses and kisses, and the intellectual challenges you gave me. I've stumbled more than once without you to hold me up. And there've been many times when I've had something to share and no one to share it with. I haven't met anyone who comes close to you. And, I too think maybe someday...But, I also know that I'm growing in ways I couldn't have grown with you. It's hard to see sometimes, but I know it's true. And I know you too are growing in ways you couldn't have with me. If we're not growing, we couldn't grow together and would have been living a lie. If we reunite let's do it when we are both flourishing not despairing.

I am considering pursuing journalism grad school. I plan on at least taking the preliminary steps: studying for the GRE's, getting information from Columbia, Michigan, UNC, Madison, etc. If I go it will probably be a year from this September. I'm feeling old and would like to have some definite course of action by then. Your advice is well intended and well received, but, to take the attitude of someone I know who watches the sun set over the ocean, doing what you love is the most important thing of all. We'll see.

I enjoyed your letters and am sorry to respond so infrequently. I too think of you often. I feel very good about our relationship now. We're more supportive than ever right now and it feels very healthy. I wish you sweet dreams and happiness.

love always,

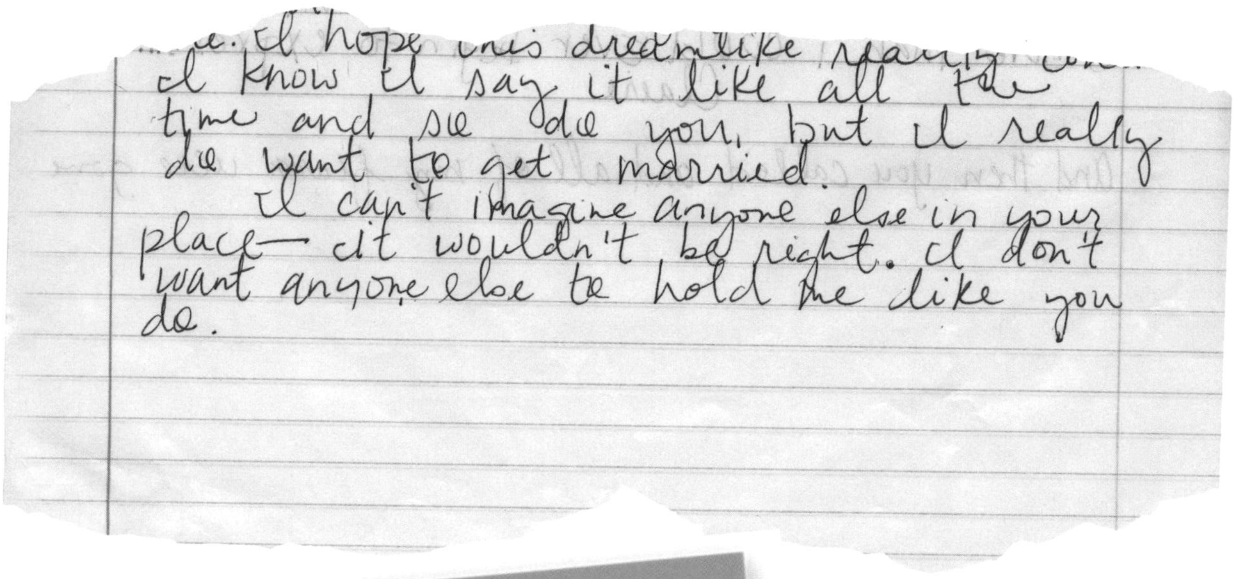

Handwritten note:

...e. I hope this doesn't like many... I know I say it like all the time and I do love you, but I really do want to get married. I can't imagine anyone else in your place— it wouldn't be right. I don't want anyone else to hold the like you do.

Phone screen:

1X

Sometimes i wish u wuz pregnant with my baby.

BACK   MORE

Email:

just remember   Inbox
More options   Aug 10

to me

just remember that as crazy as all this is, i've gotten to see a little bit of who you are and i love you. just for that. not for being anything. just you.

xo

me

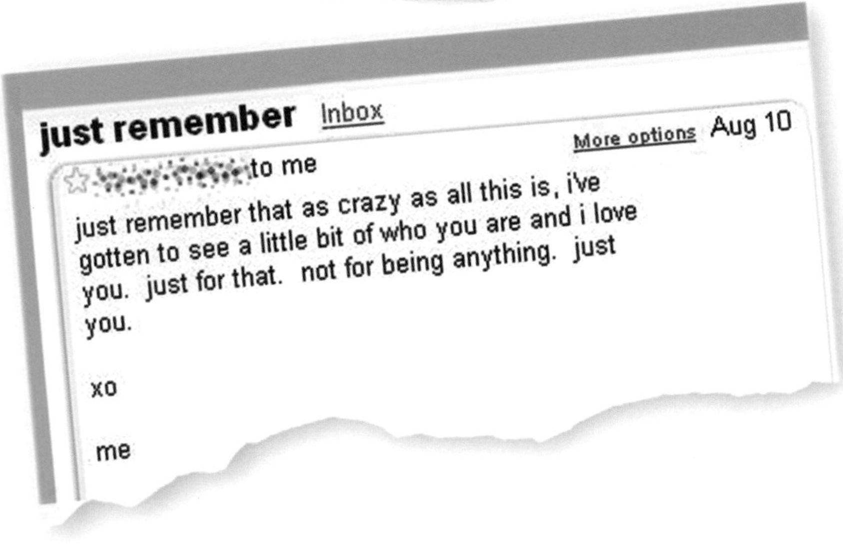

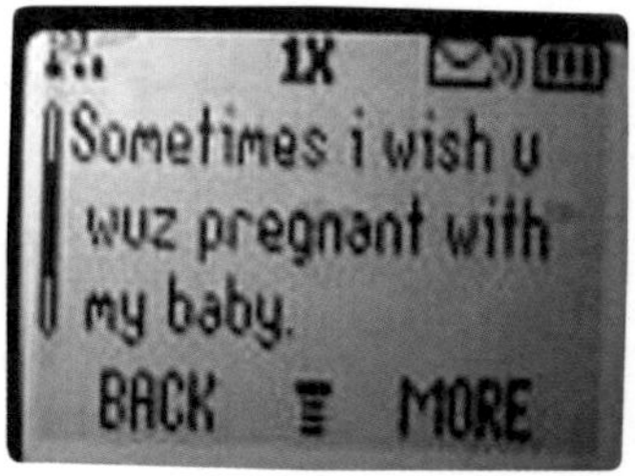

Subj: (no subject)
Date: 10/2/2005 10:25:46 PM Pacific Standard Time
From:
To:

Dearest Vicki:

Both of us know what tomorrow is and what it might be. Just in case it isn't what either of us really expects, it is important to me that you know that I love you. You have been so wonderful for me for the past 23 plus years and almost 20 full years as my wife. Thanks for all of it.

Love,

Bernard, Bunny et al.

Suffice it to say I loved you) was restless
of watching you shuffle yourself with
of watching feeling my blood burning
the skin; you wanted to examine I am
at three days of bedtime first
your own through (I) wanted so ...
I like girls and ... I am
and reflect and ...

Hi,

I agree with you about the familiarity of the
proceedings...this is the same conversation, more or less,
that we have been having for what is it? 2 1/2 years? It's
fucking awful. Not the least because it is always
destabilizing...it just never loses its bite. I am so, so
exhausted by it, literally and figuratively. Last night
was another classic example of insomnia over this impasse
on my end.

I don't have much else to say at the moment. I hope we can
work this out. It was so damn wonderful feeling so good
about our prospects. Let's try to reclaim it. We need to
figure something out, though, because I don't think I can
handle having this come up with such regularity.

Let me tell you what I wish. I wish that we could just both disappear from where we are now and be in a cuccoon. I wish I could spent every minute of what time I have left with you. I wish that I could just fall into you and dream the dream of pure love with you forever. I wish that I could make you feel things that you never knew existed. I would just want to be beside you, holding you and loving you. I have never felt this way in my life, and I think how ironic it is now that we are both entering the final quarter of our lives. Neither of us know how much time God has planned for us. I guess that is the scariest part to me. If I could somehow know that in 2, 3 5 or even ten years from now, He would arrange for us to be together, I could make it...but we don't get those kind of answers in life. Do we do what we both know is the right thing and hope that God will favor us? These are questions that I am yearning to know. It's been a long tough day for me, as I have been wrestling with these issues all day in my mind. I imagine in my fantasy world, what it would be like to come home to you each day. Would our life together get old after a while? It's hard for me to believe it would. After all it's been 30 years, and it's like we have both rediscovered the same feelings that existed so long ago, except now they are so much more intense. They have to be real and special and from our hearts where Christ resides.

```
<head>
<title> Valentines Day Card </title>
</head>

<body bgcolor="#FF000" text="FF00FF">

<SCRIPT language=javascript type="text/javascript">
    date="February 14";
    name="DanLee";
    you="my valentine";
    DanLee="you";
    if(dat=e="February 14")
    {
        if(name=="DanLee")
        {
            if(DanLee=="you")
            {
                if(you=="my valentine")
                {

                document.write("Happy Valentines Day");
                }
            }
        }
    }
//- ->end of card
</SCRIPT>
</body>
</html>
```

something happened in the last 8 months. you became my closest friend, but i also developed strong feelings for you. now you're gone, yet i still see you and think of you everywhere. i have to readjust to life without someone on whom i had relied pretty strongly for emotional support. it's shaping up to be quite a feat, seeing as your presence had helped me adjust to life here in the first place. whenever something was bothering me throughout the course of the day, i was always satisfied in knowing that i'd go home and see you and i'd feel better. that notion always helped me get through the day. this is probably coming as a shock to you, but just bear with me.

i had really started to get past this once you left in july. the first week was definitely a struggle. but then i went to boston and was doing fun things, so my mind started to be occupied. and by the time you came back from s. america and i spoke with you on the phone, i felt like i had gotten over you and you were just my very good friend, nothing more. and then i saw you again. and everything that was there came rushing back.

as sara said last night, not only is it difficult for me to handle change, i especially have difficulty going from "more to less": i had this very-close-to-ideal living situation, and now i suddenly don't. in addition to that, it's sometimes hard for me to see the forest for the trees -- i have much to focus on right now, and i now have the perfect opportunity to care for and tend to myself and my responsibilities and the things i want to do since i no longer have someone around whose well-being i sometimes considered before my own. but all i can see right now is the absence of you.

i also have trouble with the notion that i *need* to get over this. that just kills me. i don't understand why I should have to get over you. i keep telling myself that i have to and forcing myself to make it happen, but that just doesn't seem fair to me. i've spent the past few years of "growing up" realizing that i have to be much more guarded when it comes to men. i too easily allow myself to become emotionally open to men and start to care about them, some more than they have deserved. so i've really come to be much more selective. and here i found someone who is completely deserving of everything i have to offer, and we still can't be together. and i know that. definitely not now, probably not in the future either. but how is that right? what learning am i to take away from this? yes, i have a wonderful friend whom i look up to and from whom i have already learned so much. but i still don't know how to guard myself against this happening in the future. how can i start to emotionally guard myself from someone who seems so perfect for me?

I really do understand that nothing can be done with this on your part, and i don't really expect you to make it better or to respond in any certain way. it's probably almost better if you didn't. i just had to get it out. please know that i certainly don't feel in any way hurt by you -- you clearly have never hurt me. and i suspect that after reading this, you're probably inclined to want to fix it or make it better, which is a perfect example of what it is about you that i love so much. but i know it can't be fixed. it's just something with which i have to deal.

you

m

me feel

ake

free!

7/3/02

I've been thinking a lot about our ~~are~~ arguments this summer. I thought I should share my thoughts w/ you, since I always advocate ~~for~~ complete honesty. We still have quite a lot to learn about each other, especially why, how and what we are thinking. While we aren't getting along well, I think (and hope) that we are growing more now than ~~we ever have before~~ ~~XXXXXX~~

And just to let you know, I still sometimes find myself staring at you and feeling that God could not have crafted a more beautifully sweet angel, and oh how undeserved I am when I hold you.

I love you,

Cheerio16: do you remember the first time I told you I love you?
Kloudnine1: in person?
Cheerio16: yeah
Kloudnine1: yeah
Cheerio16: when?
Kloudnine1: at my aunt's house in the driveway after our first date when we were dating
Cheerio16: when it was really col
Kloudnine1: cold?
Cheerio16: yeah :-)
Kloudnine1: i was wearing my green fleece
Cheerio16: and i remember driving back to her house talking
Kloudnine1: and the windows were all down
Cheerio16: and it was cold and windy
Kloudnine1: and it was easy
Cheerio16: yes
Kloudnine1: one of my clearest memories from last year
Cheerio16: one of many

hint hint ➘

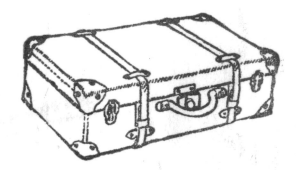

Visit Soon!

1-19-98
MLK Day

Dear ⬛-

Thank you for your thoughtful letter. It took courage to write that!
I appreciate your sharing your thoughts with me, and I hope we
can speak more — and face to face. I apologize for not responding
sooner, but both work deadlines and my emotions prevented me
from doing so until now.

I am pleased that you feel so deeply for ⬛ and that you
care for her so much. It is not my intention to interfere with
your relationship and it's many dimensions — friendship, romance,
companionship — except for one: intimacy. And there, on that
one level, I have concern for your choices and actions.

At the risk of causing you to shut me off, I must be
honestly blunt and let you know I think you are both making
a huge mistake in the new direction you've chosen in
your relationship, and I don't see any good in it.
If you truly love ⬛, you would make it your top
priority to protect her and guard her from harm or
trouble. Instead you agree to an action that puts
her in a very dangerous place — she could be subject
to extreme physical and emotional consequences as a
result of your actions. She could be subject to disciplinary
actions by the school, which would lead to great hurt
and embarrassment not only for her but for her Dad
and for me. She could be subjected to ridicule by her
classmates (regardless of what you may think — kids
can be just as hypocritical as adults!). Why would
you want to put her in such a precarious position?
For your decision and actions could easily place her in
any of these situations.

True love always places the other first. If you truly love ~~a~~ ████ please put her ahead of your ~~for~~ own desires and wishes. Please do what is best for her. That is the mark of a selfless heart. I am not implying that you've made this decision on your own – I know you both talked and decided. But I am simply asking you to consider how much danger your actions place on her – much moreso than on you (think Biologically here, in particular).

True love calls for honor, self-sacrifice, and self-denial. Mature love is able to conquer this for the sake of the relationship. Immature love grasps for everything and thus – arms overfull – loses all in the end.

In your letter you say "I know that you and ████ have a great relationship and I don't want this situation to blemish it or deny me of having a relationship with you..." If you truly mean what you say, then you will have no trouble doing what I ask of you: STOP. Because if you continue, you will just keep hurting my relationship with ████ more and more —— it's already been painfully blemished by your actions. And if you truly want to have a relationship with me (and I hope you do!) then again, the way to accomplish this is in one word: STOP. Do not continue the action you have taken – GO BACK! Stop and go back. That's all I ask. If you are able to do this, then I will know that you really do care for ████. If you choose to ignore me, then I will know not to trust you. The decision is yours. I am so hoping to meet and talk with you more about this. I know that probably sounds scary to you! But how else can we understand each other if we don't speak openly and honestly to each other?

I hope you don't mistake my firmness for dislike. I want to like you, to understand you. But you must remember one key thing: no one loves ____ more than I do! So I am just very concerned that you will do right by her, that you will honor and care for her.

I wish you well. I wish you peace. I wish you wisdom and God's deep grace. Like ripples on a pond when you throw a stone — your actions affect all in it's path. May your actions be brave and true.

With affection & Respect —

**Mail Center
Read Mail**

Bright Idea: [Read the Bulletins your friends post. **View Bulletins.**]

From: Paul

sts
ests

Date: Aug 1, 2006 12:19 PM   Flag spam/abuse [?]

Subject: :)

Smile, baby, and dream. You and me in a soft bed, no alarms, no weekdays, no commutes. I watch your breasts rise and fall with your breath, and wrap my arms around you, and hold you close, and tell you what you already know- I love you- over and over again. Because I do :)

Body:

xoxoxoxo
paulbear

<< Previous   Next >>

(-Reply-) (-Forward-) (-Save-) (-Delete-)

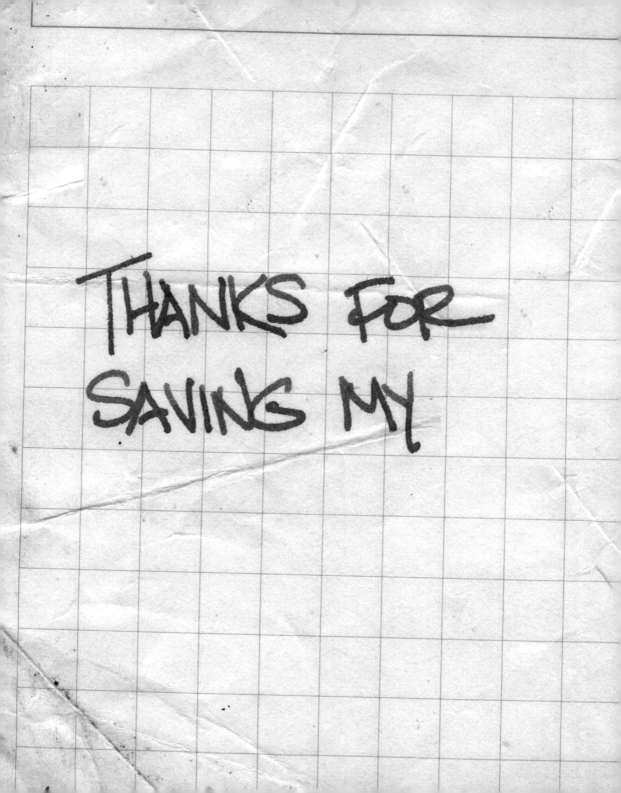

ONCE AGAIN
BURNT·OUT SOUL

Hello Cheryl,   August 3, 1976
    What's happening? Yeah, this is
Ricky, the guy that was so anxious to
write!
    I guess I should start by telling
you about myself. Even though I sent
a picture I mind as well tell you
what I look like, my height is 5'11",
brown hair and blue eyes.
    Before I say anymore you'd
better sit down and relax cause this
is going to be a rather long letter.
    As far as what kind of
personality I have, I really don't
know, but if it helps alot of people
call me & Jim brothers. Plus of the
fact he and I are always around
each other. I'm also a very
affectionate person and I can be
rather forward at times. (Like I
said, at times).
    I graduated from St. Louis
High School of Hawaii, this sounds
rather wierd but it's rather a
long story to explain.
    I have a father, 4 sisters and
one brother. I just thought I'd
just give you a more or less

of an idea of what kind of family I come from. Of course Jim told you that I come from Dartmouth, Mass. And the fact that I have 4 months left in the corps. (I can't wait for that day.)

Cheryl, I don't know what kind of letter you would call this but I'm not used to writing girls I haven't really met. So, I hope you'll bear with me. Okay

In case your wondering, I was engaged once, (a year ago) but I'd rather not go into details about a past thing.

Beleive it or not, I live about 15 minutes away from your house. I guess it was fortunate to meet Jim. Jim and I have already made plans of me going to pick him up at the airport next year, I imagine we'll always be fiends.

You wouldn't beleive some

of things your brother and
I have done.

I found out a little about
you before I wrote, and Cupid
has come to the conclusion that
you and I would get along
great. (But don't tell him).

Well, Cheryl I don't think
I should make this letter much
longer, cause I don't like
getting bored either! HA HA
I don't know what kind of
ending I should put, maybe
you know, but for now I'll
just have to sign my name.

Ricky

Jane:

Look, I'm incredibly confused. You seem very clear-headed about all this and I truly admire that. But I'm messed up. That may seem hard to understand, but it's where I am. I need a moment.

I'm aware that my taking a long breath probably feels bad to you, and I'm sorry, ~~about that~~. I truly, truly am. But I need to take it. I also need to talk to someone, and given the personal nature of this, the only person I feel comfortable talking to is my shrink. She's fitting me in tomorrow. I have a lot of feelings that I need to sort out, some involve you but most of it is about me. What happened on Thursday played into my biggest demons—trust being the biggest.

I wanted to see you tomorrow in the hope that we (me, anyway) could get some clarity from all this. That was this morning. Now I just feel like running away. (I'm being really honest here.) It feels weird to me that this seems so straightforward for you but is really fucking with my head. (I've barely slept for the last two nights.) I don't mean that as a criticism but it makes me feel like I'm over-reacting, and that only reinforces my need for the long breath. So as of now, I actually don't know how I feel about tomorrow.

I'm sorry I can't call you now.

By the way, I don't think either of us are the people we were before Thursday. Not necessarily worse, but I do feel like a layer was peeled away. As for me, ~~I feel like~~ I've shown a side of myself that's probably a major turn-off.

I'll call you tomorrow. And thanks for your notes; they mean a lot.

FEB 14

Happy Valentine's Day
to a sweet, Beautifull, intelligent, nervous, Kind, Shapley, Tall and slim, Innocent, Sexy, Friend

I "♥" U
(your house) Maximum "Babe"

love
Nico Karl

RACHEL

My heart is always there for you.

Happy 1½ Birthday

You "Melt Me"!!!

(I'll always remember when you "start")

25 more days →

July 23, 1992

Hi baby—
    I miss you!
    I haven't talked to you for 2 days! That's two days too long!
    How are you doing?
    Right now I am studying for my BIG FINAL tonight. I am reading the chapter on Interpersonal attraction and all I can think of is you.
    Well, here's some definitions ~~tea~~ for us:

    <u>Passionate love</u>: An intense and often unrealistic emotional response to another person. It is interpreted by the individuals involved as "love".

well, we do have passionate love, but we also have ↓

    <u>companionate love</u>: Love that rests on a firm base of friendship, common interests, mutual respect, and concern for the other person's happiness and welfare.

My book say companionate love is the best kind & it is the love that keeps a relationship going. I think we have strong companionate love, what do you think?
    I guess I should get back to studying! I love you!

        ♡ Sally ☺

Ok…The main thing I want to say, I've wanted to say for a little while, but I've been too scared to, because this all started out as my fault and I didn't want to look like an asshole by putting any blame on you…but I need to say it.

The last two conversations you didn't even say I love you back, you just muttered and put down the phone. How does that help me "get better"? I feel like I'm doing a lot better, and I've made progress. (its not that I want a pat on the back or a good job sticker….cause I wouldn't deserve that anyway) I don't know why its a problem, but it is and try as I might, I haven't been able to change all at once…

But onto what I really wanted to say.

When I'm here, I feel like I don't get any credit, and that makes it hard. I feel like sometimes you are just humoring me…I kid about you about being unsupportive, but sometimes I do feel unsupported, like no one has my back. Almost like, you do things for me out of this feeling of responsibility and for no other reason…

I hope I don't regret saying this, but….I've always said I don't know how to be your boyfriend here…I've come to realize that, in different ways, you don't know how to be my girlfriend there either. …and that's ok. Its contrary to what we know. We shouldn't be good at being apart. maybe none of that makes any sense, but i'm not gonna edit it. let it stand. I'm not doubting your love for me, or mine for you or this relationship or anything to that nature. This is purely distance problem. And I also whole-heartedly admit that it started with my shitty communication, and thus its my fault. But I can't help feeling the things in the above paragraph…I'm not mad at you, and if you are mad at me, fair enough. But I guess the whole point here is that we both (probably me more than you, but still) need work at this. I know that you have never claimed to be perfect, but it took me until recently to realize that you're not. I always say that when there is a problem, between us I want it out in the open, so with this email I'm practicing what I preach. …or maybe I'm just full of shit and shouldn't feel anything i said in the previous paragraphs….but there it is. for better or much worse I love you, I still, despite all, most definitely want to marry you.

Subj: **hola**
Date: 05/05/2000 8:32:47 AM Eastern Daylight Time
From: ▓▓▓▓▓
To: ▓▓▓▓▓

Sweetie, I havent had the chance to write you in a really long time, but I finally have a few minutes today, so I wanted to at least make sure I tell you I love you. I want you to know that I am glad that sometimes we have our little fights, and that it just means that we are being real with each other. That first little bit of a relationship is fun, but it isnt real, sometimes people dissagree and they fight, and sometimes they get on each others nerves. My favorite rule of management is that you have to make sure that you are making enough mistakes, otherwise you just arent trying hard enough. That same thing goes for love. I love that you make me want to be a better person, I love that you make me want to try to look better, be smarter, richer, stronger... You inspire me to greatness and to be who I am, and you inspire me to inspire you. Each day, I can feel us getting stronger, going further, understanding more. I stand behind you in each decision you make, even when I disagree. I see and appreciate all the great things that you do for me, and I hope you always remember that. I notice every little thing about you. Sometimes that can be annoying I know, but most of the time I am just seeing the way that you look at me, or the way that you go that extra mile to make me happy. I guess I should stop writing eventually, or this thing will go on forever, but sweetie, I really love you.
Te amo
  Hoy
    Manana
      Siempre
  Con todo el corazon y todo el cuerpo

CALL ME

Ken:

I would definitely advise you to cultivate your courting skills. Months of emailing do not a relationship make. I knew you liked me and I liked you too. When you first resurfaced, I urged (I would even go so far as to sayegged) you many times to see me, but you were very stubborn. I was very open at that time to seeing you and was disappointed that you wouldn't.

To wit: It took you two months to make a date.

I did not consider that a relationship, and had no way of knowing what intentions you had.

It's true that I was not seeing anyone over the summer (at the time of the infamous international dumping). But I had met someone by chance exactly three days before you resurfaced. I didn't know where that would go, and I didn't feel ready to close any doors. You never exactly stepped up. In the meantime, the other thing has progressed to an intimate and exclusive level, and it feels right.

I agree that I was a chicken shit with you at the end. I'm sorry if I hurt you. I didn't realize the extent of your feelings at all. So I think the lesson you take away is the right one. I also think that you truly are afraid of me, and I'm not sure that's the best foundation to build upon.

I enjoyed spending time with you too. And I know I will miss you.

Maria

G🔒ail™
+talk🔊   **BETA**

	Search Mail	Search the Web	Show search options
			Create a filter

Compose Mail

Kiss - findinfotoday.com/kissing - Become a Hot Kisser With These Secret Kissing Tips

Inbox (201)

Starred ☆

Chats 💬

Sent Mail

Drafts (12)

All Mail

Spam (11)

Trash

Contacts

▼ Quick Contacts

Search, add, or invite

Set status her ▼

Add
contact   Show all

▼ Labels

10/8/04

9/15/04 Clips

« **Back to Inbox**   Archive   Report Spam   Delete   More actions... ▼

I don't know what got   Inbox

☆ ▬▬▬▬▬▬ to me   More options   11:53 am (2 hours ago)

I don't know what got me higher last night all the herb we smoked or our kiss. We're gonna have to try both again so i can be sure. ;)

Reply   Forward   Invite ▬▬▬▬ @vtext.com to Gmail

Hopefully you are fast asleep as I write this...I'm
sometimes really at a loss to figure out how we can get out
of our conflicts over the phone. I know that the primary
concern is my problem with sex. I of course have my own
concerns about the sex stuff (what it means for me...why it
interests me
etc...is there a way that I can be kinder to you outside of
a
moratorium....maybe not...so it's You vs Sex..decide!).
In addition I feel like our conversations easily become a
broken record with no way of either of us seeing a way to
move the needle, and start the song again or maybe just
skipping ahead to a new song. I also wonder about some of
your qualities at times and ultimately whether we can
manage or even should
manage a meaningful relationship. How compatable we are...
It feels like such work sometimes.

Having said all of that I always seem to be left with the
realization that we have this unusually intense soulmate
quality of love that really exists. When it is around, I
can see its power and wonder. It is hard to forget, I
doubt I ever will, but it does seem to hide...tonight is a
good example.

The good news is that our love seems to return with an
intensity that I can still remember when I first saw you
walking down the concourse in seattle. It happened last
weekend and I am confident it will return. Do you think
so?

Hey babe. I hope you are feeling better. I enjoyed our conversation a lot last night. I never thought that we would have so much to say despite the fact we haven't met yet!!

I see so much in you -- so much that I have been waiting to see in someone. It's like all your life you dream of the ideal person who will just complete your heart in every way. And you think to yourself, does this ideal person even exist? Along the way you meet all the wrong ones and it kinda brings you down, but you try to just keep your head up and your heart open.

I think I've always been yearning for love. It's like even when I had boyfriends, I was still lonely, because they could never fill this void in my heart. I wanted them to so badly, but they were totally wrong for me, and I knew I could do so much better. It's just everything about love and sharing yourself with another human being that is so intimate and special and rare.

There's something about you that I can't place. It's like you amaze me everytime. Honestly, I've never known anyone quite like you. It's a bit scary, but at the same time you give me this reassurance that maybe, just maybe, YOU are that ideal person; the person who will make my heart complete.

I thank you so much for making me smile and just being the person that you are. You're such an amazing guy! And I really mean that. I can't wait to meet you to see what happens. Talk to you later.

-Jen-

anyone.

(Now I'm going to shower)

REOPENING THE ENVELOPE

A few contributors reveal how it felt to search through their closets, garages, and hard drives—through time itself—and wander into their romantic back pages. Some were overcome by warmth and nostalgia; others experienced heartbreak all over again. But nearly everyone said that, within the envelope, they found a little peace.

i regret some of what i wrote

"I thought digging up these old letters would be no big deal. I thought I'd mourned, healed, and moved on from all of my serious and not-so-serious relationships over the last ten years. But apparently not: I was completely surprised by how painful it was to look at the permanent record of all these lost loves.

"I noticed a couple of things: I'm blessed in that I have some gift with words, and that I can use words to inspire joy in someone or to comfort someone. But there's this dark side that when I'm hurt or in pain, I can draw blood with my words. And I regret some of what I wrote out of anger or hurt. I feel real shame from this. Did I cause harm to someone? I'm seriously think-ing about going back to some of these guys after all these years and apologizing."

it was first love

"I hadn't read the letters since I'd received them—that was about fifteen years ago. It was a college relationship, my first love.

"As I read them, I had this sudden desire to feel that intensity again. I wanted it back in my life *right now.* But when I thought about it, I came to realize that you can never re-create those feelings because it was the first time, the first love. And that's actually the beauty of it: If you *could* experience those feelings again, then they would be worthless.

"After I read the letters, I e-mailed her. We hadn't talked in five years. We had a laugh over our letters because they were so gooey and naïve. But I felt a little dif-ferent about them than she did: I was probably more nostalgic, more romantic."

a great honor

"My mother and I went through stacks and stacks of my grandparents' letters. They had corresponded for four years, sometimes three times a week. It was a great honor to be able to see the intricacy of their courtship and that they truly adored each other until their parting breaths. My mother and I were both touched by their love. I don't mean that in the cliché sense—we could see that their love affected all of us as developing people.

"We spent days reading and organizing them, and then my mother decided to assemble a book of all of the letters. We gave one to everyone in my family. They, too, were entranced."

who *was* i then?

"Reading them again was disorienting. You remember thinking the thoughts and writing the words but, man, you can't *touch* those feelings. It's like they belonged to someone else. Someone you don't even know. I'm aware, in an intellectual way, that I felt all of those things about her, but those emotions are far away now.

"What's so strange to me is that I can't even force my heart back to that place where I felt that all-consuming passion. That makes me feel distant from myself. Who *was* I then? Will I ever be able to get back to that place? Reading the letters again made me wonder: Which is the real me? The one who saw the world in that emotionally saturated way, or the me who sees it the way I do now?"

i cried my eyes out

"When I read a few of the letters, I just cried my eyes out. It was like I experienced the end of each relationship again."

a nice surprise

"I didn't know these letters existed. My grandmother died before I was born, so this was the first time I've ever heard her voice, heard how she constructed her thoughts. It was an amazing experience. Sometimes she seemed demanding, sometimes she seemed scared. The stories I'd heard about my grandparents were that they were so different, but to have a glimpse into their sweetness and excitement about love was a nice surprise."

my love comes in many shapes and sizes

"By going through my old letters I saw that my love comes in many shapes and sizes: Some are free-falls in a mad, passionate way. Some loves have been more friendship-based, sweeter and warmer. Looking at these letters reminded me that I've had the opportunity to experience many types of men and relationships, and that all of these romantic adventures make me who I am.

"I saw progress in how I dealt with rejection and pain over the years. When I split up with a couple of these men, I was in my closet thinking I could never come out . . . but here I am. Looking back gave me a sense that I had survived."

POSTSCRIPT

How did the lovers meet? Did they live happily ever after? Here's the story behind a few of the letters, as well as an update on how the relationship fared.

Where do you stand on chains?

The writer walked by a shop window and saw her: a beautiful sales-clerk. So he stopped in, bought something he didn't need and, quite intentionally, left his glasses on the counter. When he retuned to pick them up, he also got her e-mail address. They flirted for two weeks (exchanging dozens of notes) and dated for four months, during which time he found out exactly where she stood on chains.

Peace. Sweat. Everything!

It took her about two hours to create this illustration and, as she remembers it, perhaps a bit longer than that to pick out the perfect color of red lipstick for the pucker. The couple met in college in '92—she liked his Morrissey shirt—and have been together ever since.

I love you, Gary

The couple met on JDate. Her note was written one morning when he had to leave for work and she stayed in his bed. She knew this note would make him smile when he returned that night. She was right, and they've been married for more than two years.

Thank you, I hate you, I'm sorry

She gave this note to her boyfriend just before moving to New York City—without him. They spent two years apart—"growing up and living life," she says—but never stopped thinking about each other. Then, on his own, he moved to New York and they began seeing each other again. She says they don't for a minute regret the decisions they made—to go, to stay—that brought them to where they are now: sharing an apartment.

6:35 A.M.—Gone for my walk

Donald and Mildred were married in 1937 with only $17 in the bank. Two years after celebrating their Golden Anniversary, Don underwent open-heart surgery; unfortunately, his aorta ruptured, leaving him in a coma for two months. He awoke with compromised mental and physical abilities, but recovered enough to draw Mildred a love note before his morning walk—which he did every single day until he died, five years later.

Hi Lauren

She left her small New England university to spend her junior year at a school about an hour outside of London. Early on, she met a guy, a Brit, and was, she says, "quietly in love with him" the entire year. The night before she returned to the States, they finally kissed. As she was leaving for the plane the next morning, a mutual friend handed her this letter. They e-mailed now and then but after a couple of years fell out of touch. Recently, she was flipping through a stack of old letters, read this note, started wondering . . . and decided to reach out to him. They e-mailed about five times before he hopped on a plane. She hadn't seen him in ten years but they had "the most beautiful, romantic weekend. He's coming again soon."

Subject: money and house stuff

Molly and her husband divorced after eight years of marriage. Both are in relationships now and they remain friends.

You sure looked good in those sweats

Chris and Roz were high school sweethearts. But during his freshman year of college, Labor Day weekend of 1984, Chris was killed in a car accident. Roz has saved the note and maintained a close relationship with Chris's mother for more than twenty years.

Dear beautiful

It was another blind date; this time her uncle had set her up. The plan: Meet outside of her fancy Midtown Manhattan office building. How would she recognize him? "I'll be the guy with the hole in his boot," he told her. And there he was, covered in dust from his construction job, with a big hole in his fraying boot. What was supposed to be one drink turned into two . . . then a ride on the Ferris wheel in Toys R Us . . . then dinner. He wrote her this note exactly two months after their first date, delivering it rolled up and tied with a string, along with two red roses. They were married in July 2006.

Will you be my wife?

His girlfriend was always the photographer. She'd somehow managed to capture every one of their special occasions with a Polaroid—their first New Year's Eve together, holding hands on a trampoline, the night they watched for falling stars. So it just seemed right, he thought, to capture the memory of his proposing to her. On November 5, 2005, he asked her to look for a surprise inside the drawer of a small table. While she rifled through the drawer, he got down on one knee beside her. When she finally found this Polaroid, he had the ring waiting. She looked up from the picture, and he asked her to marry him. She said yes.

Mi flor

The couple met during an intimacy exercise at a weekend workshop called "The Miracle of Love." He had just gotten out of a relationship and was more trying to figure out what went wrong than looking to meet anyone. But there she was. They've been together two years and recently held a commitment ceremony at California's Joshua Tree National Park.

Nude

This card was written several months into the couple's second attempt at a relationship. It was left for its recipient on the bed, and read in private later that evening. This time, they've been together for two and a half years. (The word "neyuwl" was, until very, very recently, one of the couple's private jokes.

On the occasion of my being made aware of the birth of our firstborn

Ellen spotted Jack at a college bar. He was a junior—and very cute. They fell in love. She became a teacher in Harlem; he became a Marine, a lieutenant. They were married in February of 1968 and moved to the base in Quantico, Virginia. She was well into her pregnancy when, in March of 1969, Jack shipped out to Vietnam. They exchanged frequent letters and audiotapes, and even talked on the phone once. Their son was born on June 6. On June 30—just a few days before he was set to leave Vietnam and see his boy for the first time—Jack was killed. Ellen saved every one of his letters and, thirty years later, their son, John Hulme, used the letters—including this one— to retrace his father's movements during the war. Ultimately, he and Ellen found the very spot in Vietnam where Jack lost his life. John made the documentary film *Unknown Soldier* about their experience.

While you were out getting stoned

This note, left on her desk by a coworker, ignited a first date for the last night of 1999. The couple married in 2004.

A year with Pooks and Dude

Judith ("Dude") created this booklet in 1970 for her husband Jonathan ("Pooks") to commemorate their first year of marriage. After thirty-seven years, they're happily married with three grown children and two grandchildren.

It's a dusty one today

This letter was sent from Iraq, where the author was flying Blackhawk helicopters. The couple met in high school, in 1977, and married in '81; they have three grown children. He's completed two tours of duty in Iraq and is expecting to return for a third.

I can't call you on your birthday

Erica Smith blogged this open letter to her boyfriend, Ben Stern, on what would have been his thirty-sixth birthday. He died of a heart attack on January 23, 2005, while the couple was walking through a park during a blizzard after midnight.

Braille

After the Great Depression, when jobs were still hard to find, a carpenter began working at a residential institution for the blind. There, he met a secretary. She was plucky and sociable, and although she had lost her sight in her early twenties, she could still type. She typed him love notes and he taught himself Braille so he could write back. He gave her this card for Valentine's Day with the card's message lovingly, if not accurately, translated in Braille and signed "love from Pete." They married and had one child, who shared this letter.

I think you know how much my life has changed

She was a summering legal intern, he was an attorney, and, yes, they met in the copy room. She was Xeroxing stacks of documents and he kept coming in to make tea. On his tenth trip for tea that morning he said "hi" and asked her to lunch; they started dating that day. The note was written at the end of her internship. They've been dating for three years.

Mr. H Goldberg: Your letter on hand

Frieda, the daughter of a rabbi, lived in Toledo, Ohio. While visiting Springfield, she met Harry, a man in his mid-twenties, who owned a small mom-and-pop grocery store. Harry's story was compelling: At sixteen, he had emigrated, by himself, from Poland to New York, where he worked in the sweatshops, and then from the sweatshops to Springfield. This note was written in response to one of his first letters to her.

Their quick courtship played out entirely on paper—they never dated before they were married, when she moved to Springfield. They lived in a house attached to the grocery store (open 7 a.m. to 9 p.m.), where they both worked. Frieda and Harry had three children and were married for fifty-eight years.

I might marry you

Jacob and Phoebe have been friends since they were infants. Both are still single.

Darling

In the mid-thirties, a traveling salesman (he specialized in jeans, boots, and Western gear) walked into a shop in Trinidad, Colorado, hoping to make a sale. When he saw a stunning young woman working at the counter, he asked her out for a Coke instead. They went on a couple of quick dates—including a boat ride on a pond where she plucked a small stone from the shore as a souvenir—before he got back on the road. He continued traveling and their courtship unfolded almost entirely by mail. They married in 1939 and remained madly in love until he died in 2001. When she died two years later, she was buried with the stone she had kept from that first boat ride.

Reasons why I love Kay

Don and Kay were married for twenty-four years. Not long after this note was written—composed, as Don says, "as a gift" —Kay was killed in a highway car accident.

Subj: (no subject)

This e-mail was written by the husband hours before he was going into surgery . . . just in case. He pulled through, and they recently celebrated their twenty-first anniversary.

Hello, Cheryl. What's happening?

Cheryl was sixteen, and living at home in Rhode Island. Ricky was in the Marine Corps stationed in Hawaii. Her brother, also in the Corps, also in Hawaii, suggested that Ricky become pen pals with his kid sister. And so they began writing back and forth . . . and back and forth. Over four months, she wrote him more than sixty letters; he wrote her more often—one a day until he was shipped home. (His very first letter is included here.) His home, as it turned out, was just thirty-five miles from where she lived. The first time they saw each other was when she picked him up at the airport. After dating for two and a half years, they were married in 1979. Every once in a while, she says, they still take out the letters—they've saved them all—and "laugh at how young we were."

Jane: Look, I'm incredibly confused.

The couple dated for two months.

Subject: Hey babe

They connected on an Internet dating site and e-mailed for a month before meeting each other. This e-mail was written a few days before their first date: She picked him up at the train station and there he was, holding a rather large bouquet of flowers. It was, she says, love at first sight. They've been together for two years.

ACKNOWLEDGMENTS

Lots and lots of people contributed to this book
(see below) but none more so than the amazing Julia Lazarus,
Daniel Souweine, and the other superhuman reporters—Teresa
Dumain, Betsy Levine, Claire Vath, Kalli Rasbury, Jen Trolio,
and Natasha Sarkisian—who corralled their friends, called
their exes, and cajoled their currents.

Thanks to my agent, Brian DeFiore; to Doris Cooper, Lauren Shakely,
Laura Palese, and Min Lee at Clarkson Potter; and to Matthew Snyder,
Jenny Sucov, Mark Jannot, Maura Fritz, and Bernard Ohanian for all of
their smart ideas. And to my family—Sasha, Soren, Mom, Dad, Vicki, Dean,
Haim, and Chris, too—who have taught me a thing or two about love.

Also, my deep gratitude to the hundreds and hundreds of people who
searched their closets and hard drives, and shared their most personal
possessions . . . as well as to those who didn't want to share but still
managed to convince their friends to do so. Without you, this book
doesn't exist: Amy Binder, Anna, Linda Permann, Paul Heaston, Barnaby,
Jason Kersten, Judy Dutton, Angela Pierce, Molly, Ryan Shipp, Sarah
Ballard, DRH, Carin Goldberg, James Biber, Jackie Mitchard, Jason Randel,
Beth, Jeffrey Ho, the family of Rebecca and Simon Goldman, Sally Kuhlman,
Jeff Nelson, Blankee, Antonia and Joseph Lombardi, Rai, Judith and
Jonathan Souweine, Jean Kwon, Ted and Rosalie Goldman, Karen Ginsburg,
Jonathan Hutchins, Basha, Peter and Esther Mazen, Erica Smith, Andrew
Steele, Phoebe Levine, Kassra Nassiri, Christin Deener, Claire and
Herbert Shapiro, John M. Burgess, Philip Dumain, Amanda Spielman,
Kristen Costa, Bill Goldman, Inma Pena, Avnish Bhatnagar, Rebecca
Lanthorne, Patrick, James Lockwood-Stewart and Barbara Stewart Hoff
(children of Donald and Mildred Stewart), Stephen Vath, KellyAnn
Kotropoulos, Lt. John William Hulme IV and Ellen Hulme, Nina Malkin,
Jason Stutts, Zach and Brooklyn, Bim Ayandele, Roslyn and Gerald
Schlenker, Johanna Womer Benjamin, Neill Livingston, Holly Lien, Adam

Schroth, Lily Byrne, Pookoos, Nikki and Larry Steen, Jennifer Pisano, Johnny Sobolewski, Justin and Blythe Jonas, Gustavo Vargas, Matt Marrone, John Michael Shimer, Don Aprill, Al Suarez, Peter Levy, Joseph Pierson, Marisa Belger, Jennifer DeLeo, Lois Berson, Philip Goldberg, Donovan and Becky Harris, Kris Mikkelson, Ann Pollack, Ella Luttbeg, Joseph Plastina, Cara R., April L. Rondeau, Nora Woolley, Chris Borris, Chris and Maureen of Baton Rouge, Trina Kaplan, Cynthia Stein, Lauren Wolfe, Zachary Byerly, Alisa Blackwood, Evelyn Martin-Anderson and Leon Anderson, Rick and Cheryl Marland, Daniel Rowles, Lesli and Greg DeMoss, Trudy Remy, Bob Mladinich, Johnathan Player, Ivan and Amy Nanola, JBI International, Monica Dzialo, Kent Wagner, and those who wished to remain nameless (you know who you are). And a special thanks to the wonderful rar rar press.

Finally, thanks to the following, who graciously permitted me to reprint their cards, designs, and words in these pages:

Card on page 113 reprinted with permission.
Hallmark Cards, Incorporated (Hallmark Licensing, Inc.)

Card on page 107
reproduced by permission.
American Greetings Corporation
© AGC, Inc.

Cards on pages 119, 136—137, 154, 160
reproduced with permission from
rar rar press
www.rarrarpress.com

Card on page 55 reprinted with permission from GoCARD
www.Gocard.com

Roche Laboratories, Inc.

"Gold," from WHITE APPLES AND THE TASTE OF STONE: Selected Poems, 1946-2006 by Donald Hall. Copyright © 2006 by Donald Hall. Reprinted by permission Houghton Mifflin Company. All rights reserved.